The magnificent Martin Baker MB.5, without doubt this aircraft reached the zenith of piston-engined fighter development and it is most unfortunate it was never placed in production, had it been it would have more than paid its way in the last few months of World War II, in the immediate post-war years in service with the RAF, and as a valuable export item to many of the world's air forces in place of the North American P-51D Mustang. In retrospect this brilliant piece of engineering could rightly be called the TSR-2 of 1945.

# 50 FIGHTERS 1938-1945

For the enthusiast or modeller interested in military aviation, few aircraft types hold quite such a fascination as does the fighter, with its undertones of individualism, lone combat, adventure and chivalry. For those who share this enthusiasm, there can surely be little more appealing, more appetite-whetting, than the rare and the unusual. The one-off prototype, the small production run model, or the well-known type in unfamiliar markings, all hold their own peculiar delights for the connoisseur... and here is a feast of such rarities!

Richard Ward has depicted here a wide selection of fighters well-supported by photographic evidence. In our first category—the one-off prototypes—are the unusual Curtiss XP-55 Ascender canard fighter, the superb Martin Baker MB.5, the Grumman XF5F-1 Skyrocket built for the U.S. Navy, and its close cousin, the U.S. Army's XP-50, as well as the Finnish V.L. Pyörremyrsky, which has recently been rebuilt by enthusiasts in that country.

In the second category are such rarities as an Avia B-135, built in Czechoslovakia but used by the Bulgarian Air Force; a Heinkel He 112 of the Rumanian Air Force (actually used operationally in the markings shown on the Russian Front), a Yugoslav Ikarus IK-3 and Rumanian IAR-81s. Amongst the more well-known aircraft of the third category are a number of unusual and different schemes; the Russian Hurricane and Croat Fiat G.50bis; the Bulgarian PZL P-24, the Rumanian-built and operated Messerschmitt Bf 109G, and the Allison-engined North American P-51A Mustang with its unidentified "Sharks' Teeth" in China.

The majority of the fighters depicted here actually saw combat painted in the style and insignia shown. For many this period of action was short and often obscure; for others it was long and distinguished. The General Motors FM-2 for instance was but the last in the long line of Grumman Wildcat variants to see service, flying from the smaller escort carriers in both Pacific and Atlantic long after the decks of larger vessels had become crowded with more potent Hellcats and Corsairs. That included here was still operational against the Japanese as late as spring 1945.

Some—the Mitsubishi A5M, the Morane 406, the Curtiss Hawk 75A and the Fiat G.50bis—represent the early days of the low-wing monoplane fighter, while others—the Martin Baker MB.5, the Kawanishi N1K2-j, the Reggiane Re.2005 and the Pyörremyrsky—represent the very peak of piston-engine fighter development. The PZL P-24 stands alone midway between biplane and monoplane, by 1938 an interesting and attractive anachronism.

**Caudron C.714
Polish Air Force**

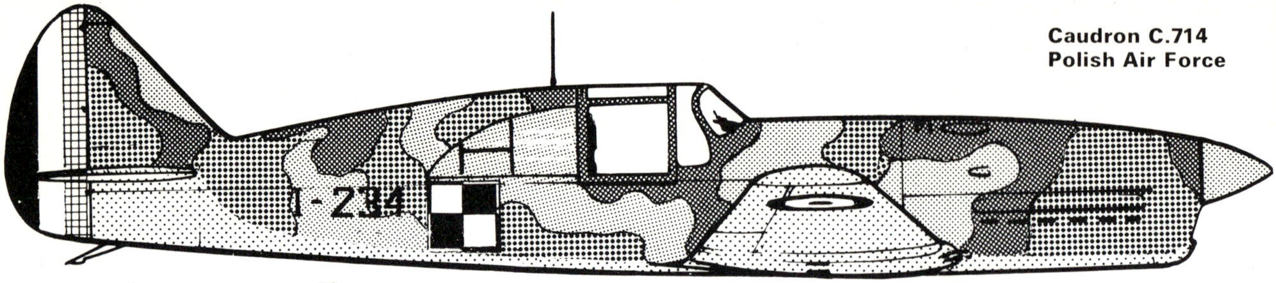

A3
Starboard side details.

- Brown
- Grey
- Green
- Pale Grey-blue
- Blue

**Note.**
Wing roundels standard French blue, white, red.
Red shown black.

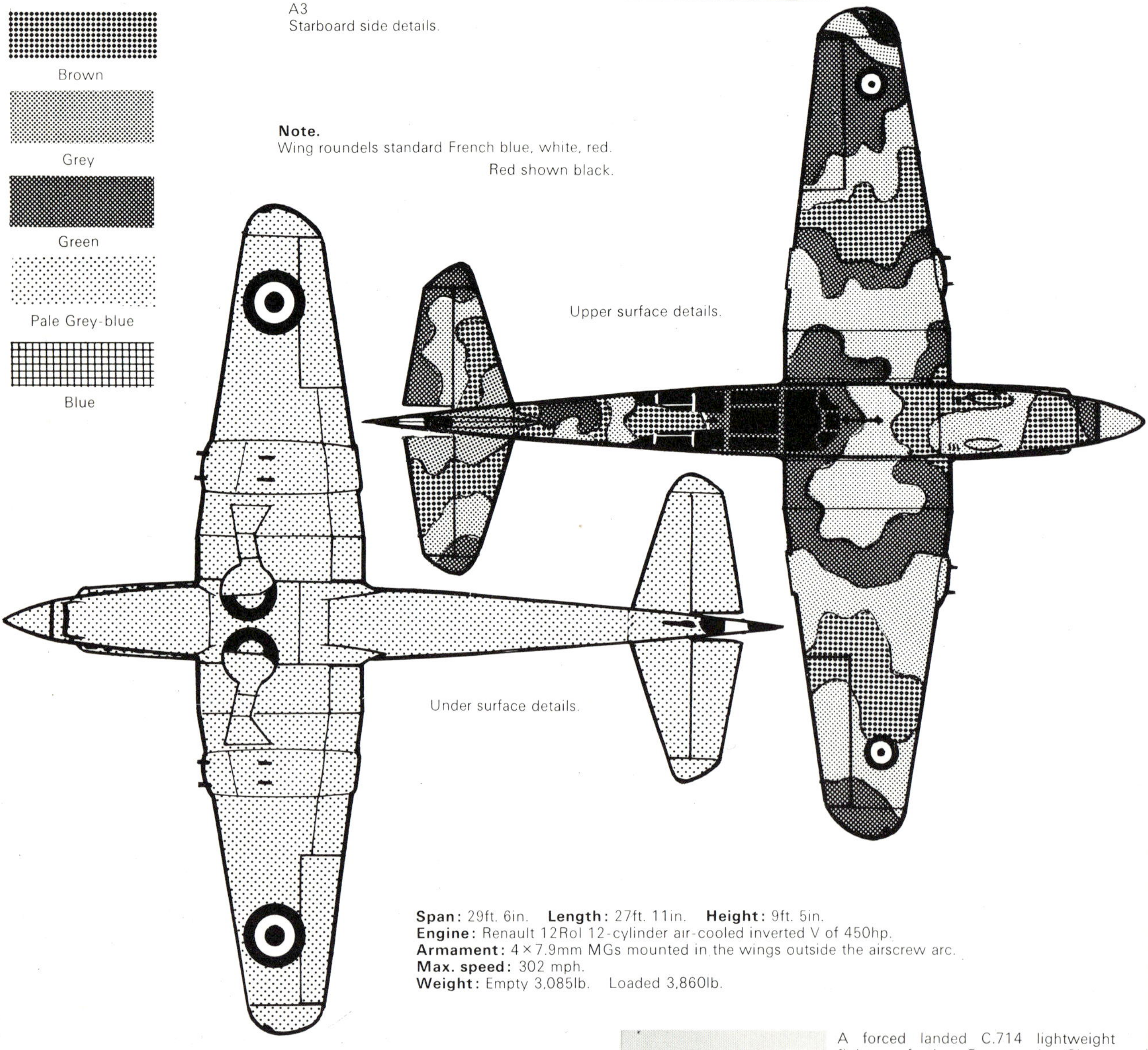

Upper surface details.

Under surface details.

**Span:** 29ft. 6in.  **Length:** 27ft. 11in.  **Height:** 9ft. 5in.
**Engine:** Renault 12Ro1 12-cylinder air-cooled inverted V of 450hp.
**Armament:** 4 × 7.9mm MGs mounted in the wings outside the airscrew arc.
**Max. speed:** 302 mph.
**Weight:** Empty 3,085lb.  Loaded 3,860lb.

A forced landed C.714 lightweight fighter of the Groupe de Chasse Polonaise de Varsovie I/145 which operated from Lyon-Bron, Dreux and Semaises airfields during May and June 1940. Operating from Dreux in early June the unit defended the Seine sector between Vernon and Menton, during the units brief period of operations it achieved 12 confirmed air victories plus two probables. (J. B. Cynk)

# AIRCAM AVIATION SERIES

**No. S.17 (VOL. 1)**

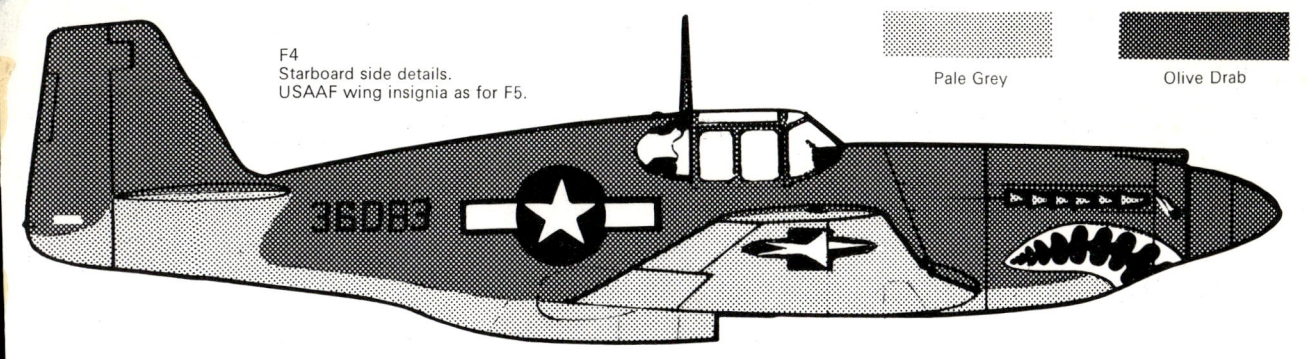

F4
Starboard side details.
USAAF wing insignia as for F5.

Pale Grey   Olive Drab

# 50 FIGHTERS 1938-1945

**Illustrated and compiled by Richard Ward**

**Introduction by Christopher F. Shores**

ACKNOWLEDGEMENTS

This series of books covering fighter aircraft of the 1938–1945 period, of which this is the first volume, will illustrate the good, the bad and the indifferent, the well known and the little known, from one- or two-off prototypes to 20,000-plus production runs. Wherever possible new or little known photographs and colour schemes will be used to illustrate the well known types. Fighter aircraft operated by neutral countries will also be covered in subsequent books. The aircraft have been arranged in alphabetical order by manufacturer's name, chronologically within that name. My thanks to all those who assisted with information and photographs.

Line-up of North American P-51A Mustangs of an unidentified unit on Kunming airfield in 1943. The shape of the teeth in the mouth are very similar to those painted on the P-40K Warhawks of the Chinese American Composite Wing late in 1943. photographic evidence indicates that no other unit used this particular design of Sharkmouth. (Herbert Rumburg)

Published by: Osprey Publishing Limited, England
Editorial Office: P.O. Box 5, Canterbury, Kent, England
Subscription & Business Office: P.O. Box 25, 707 Oxford Road, Reading, Berkshire, England

The Berkshire Printing Co. Ltd.   © Osprey Publishing Ltd. 1973 ISBN 0 85045 130 2

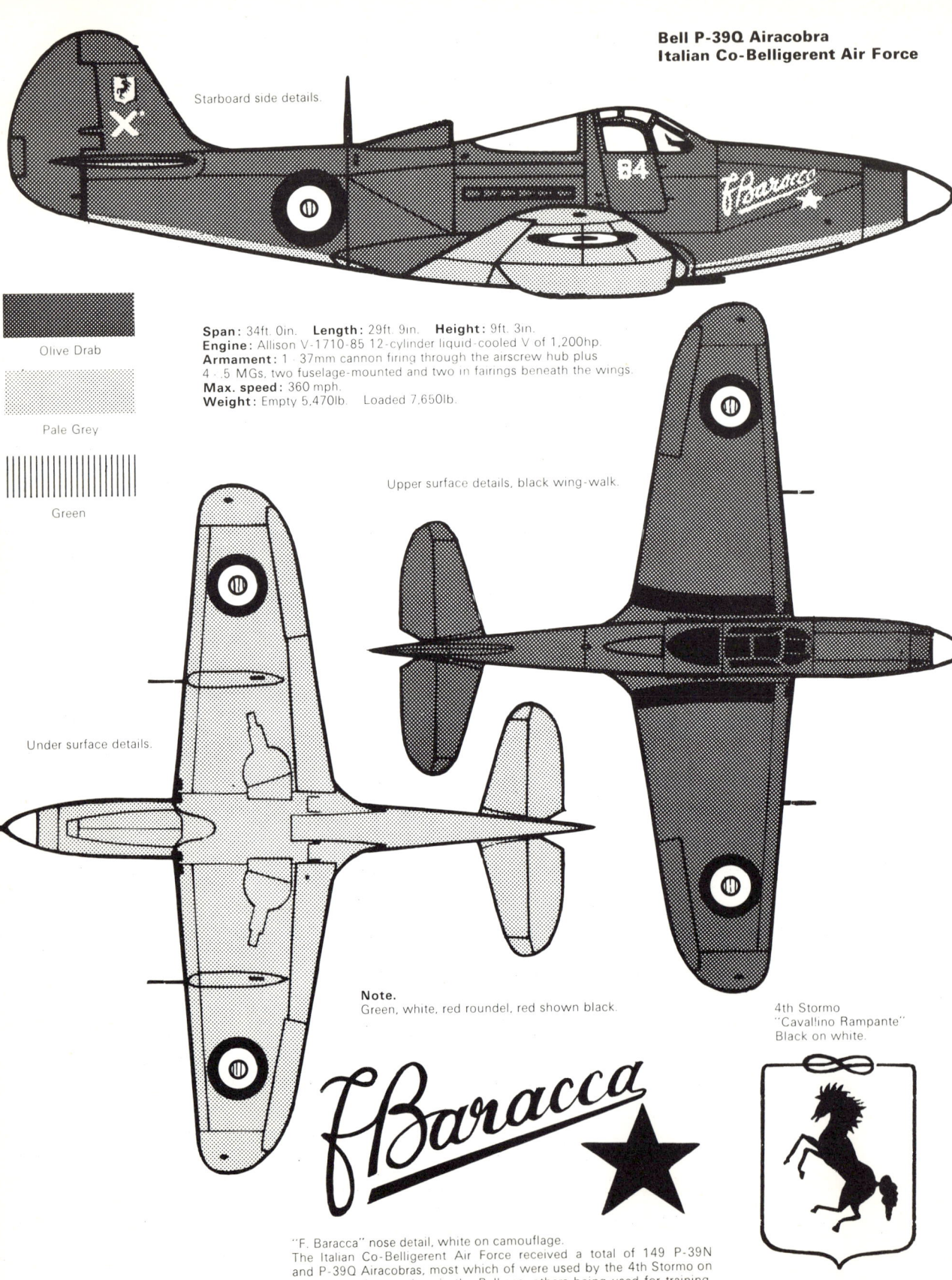

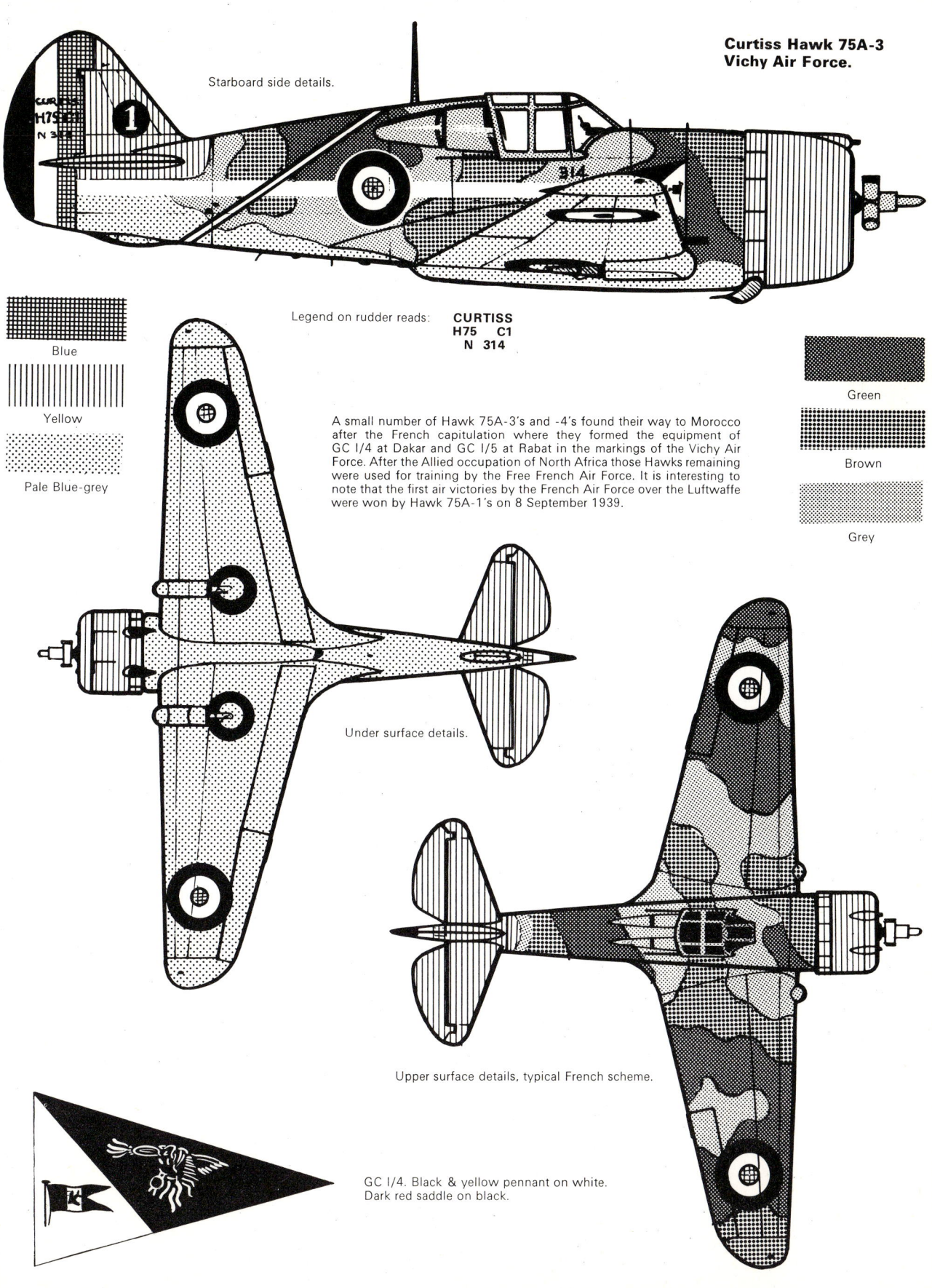

# Curtiss Hawk 75A-7
## Netherlands East Indies Air Force

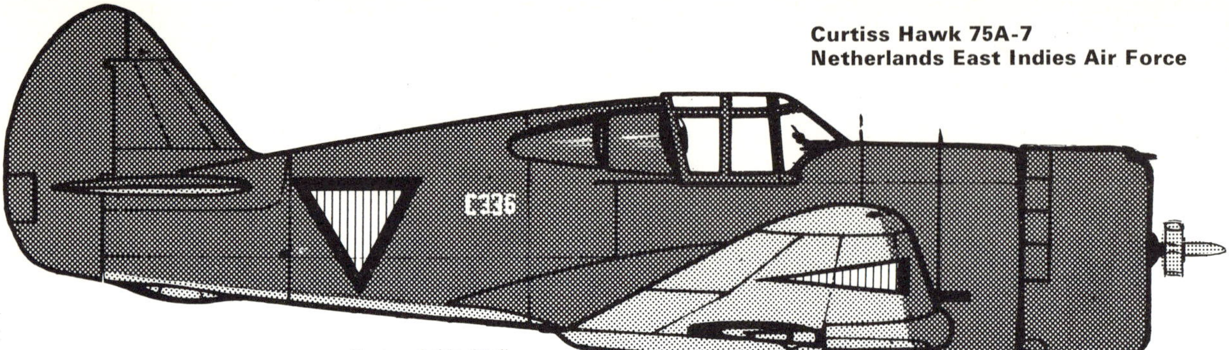

Starboard side detail.

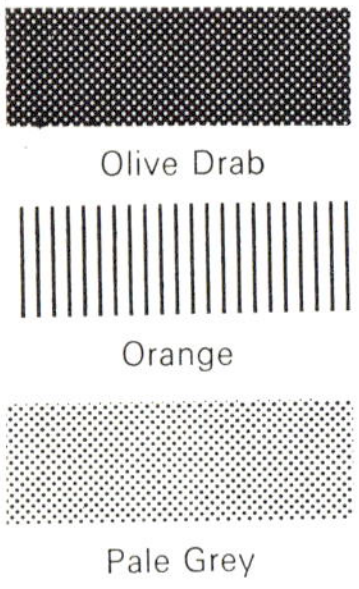

Olive Drab

Orange

Pale Grey

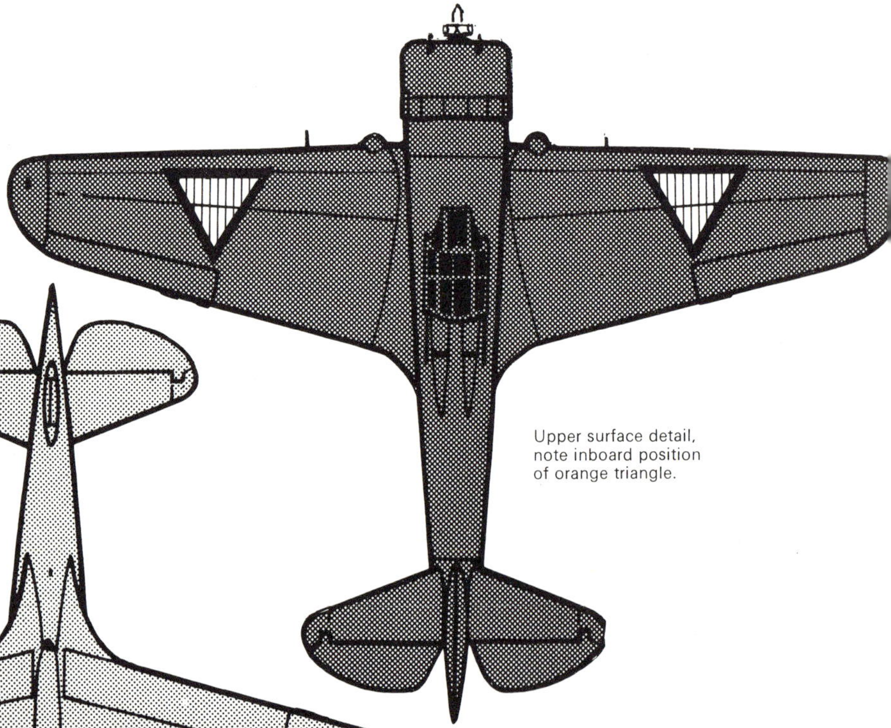

Upper surface detail, note inboard position of orange triangle.

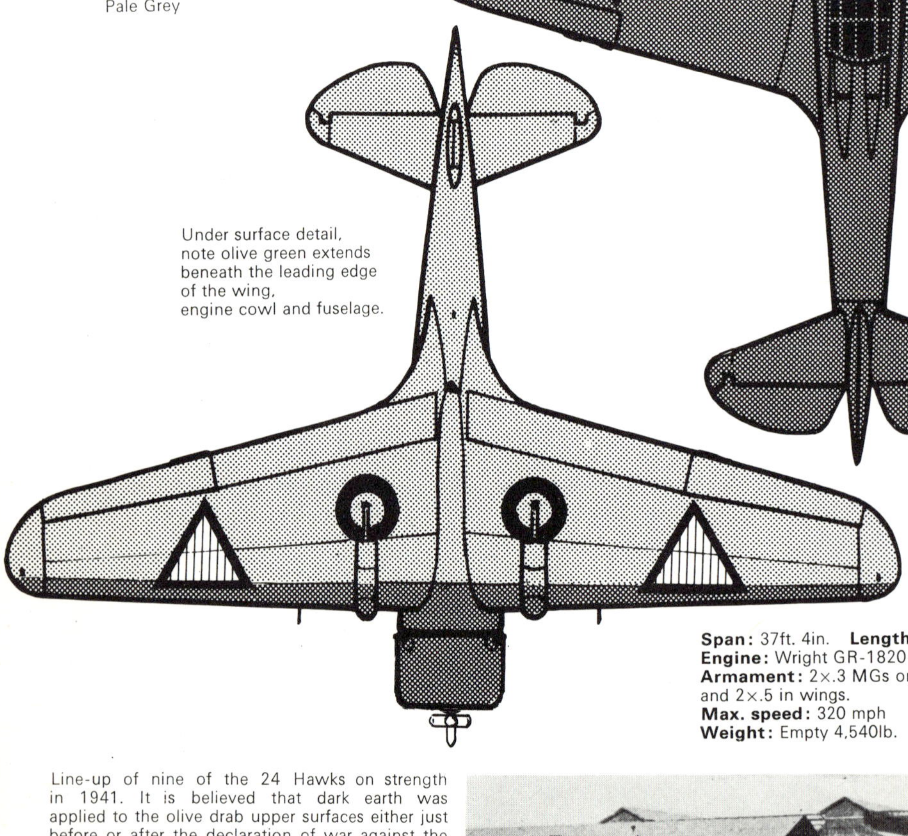

Under surface detail, note olive green extends beneath the leading edge of the wing, engine cowl and fuselage.

**Span:** 37ft. 4in. **Length:** 28ft. 6in. **Height:** 9ft. 6in.
**Engine:** Wright GR-1820-G205A Cyclone 9 of 1,200hp.
**Armament:** 2×.3 MGs on top deck of fuselage firing through airscrew and 2×.5 in wings.
**Max. speed:** 320 mph
**Weight:** Empty 4,540lb. Loaded 5,750lb.

Line-up of nine of the 24 Hawks on strength in 1941. It is believed that dark earth was applied to the olive drab upper surfaces either just before or after the declaration of war against the Japanese. The pattern is not known but may have been similar to that applied to the CW 21B's. (via G. H. Kamphuis)

Right: A loose formation of NEIAF Hawk 75A-7's, clearly shown is the position of the orange triangle and white serial on the fuselage.

Right: Nose detail, note the serial, C336 in black on the leading edge of the wing.

Out of an original order for 35 Hawk 75A-7's placed by the Netherlands government for service with the R.Neth.AF a total of 24 were diverted to the Netherlands East Indies after the German occupation of the Low Countries. The 24 Hawks were delivered in 1940 and had reached operational status by the time of the Japanese invasion. Flying alongside the Curtiss-Wright CW-21B and Brewster 339D the Hawks gave a good account of themselves for the brief period of fighting before the capitulation.

Below: Line-up of Hawk 75A-7's obviously taken before 8 December 1941 when the Netherlands declared war on the Japanese and dispersal became the order of the day. Note natural metal airscrews and that the second and fourth aircraft do not have wing guns. (Photos via G. H. Kamphuis)

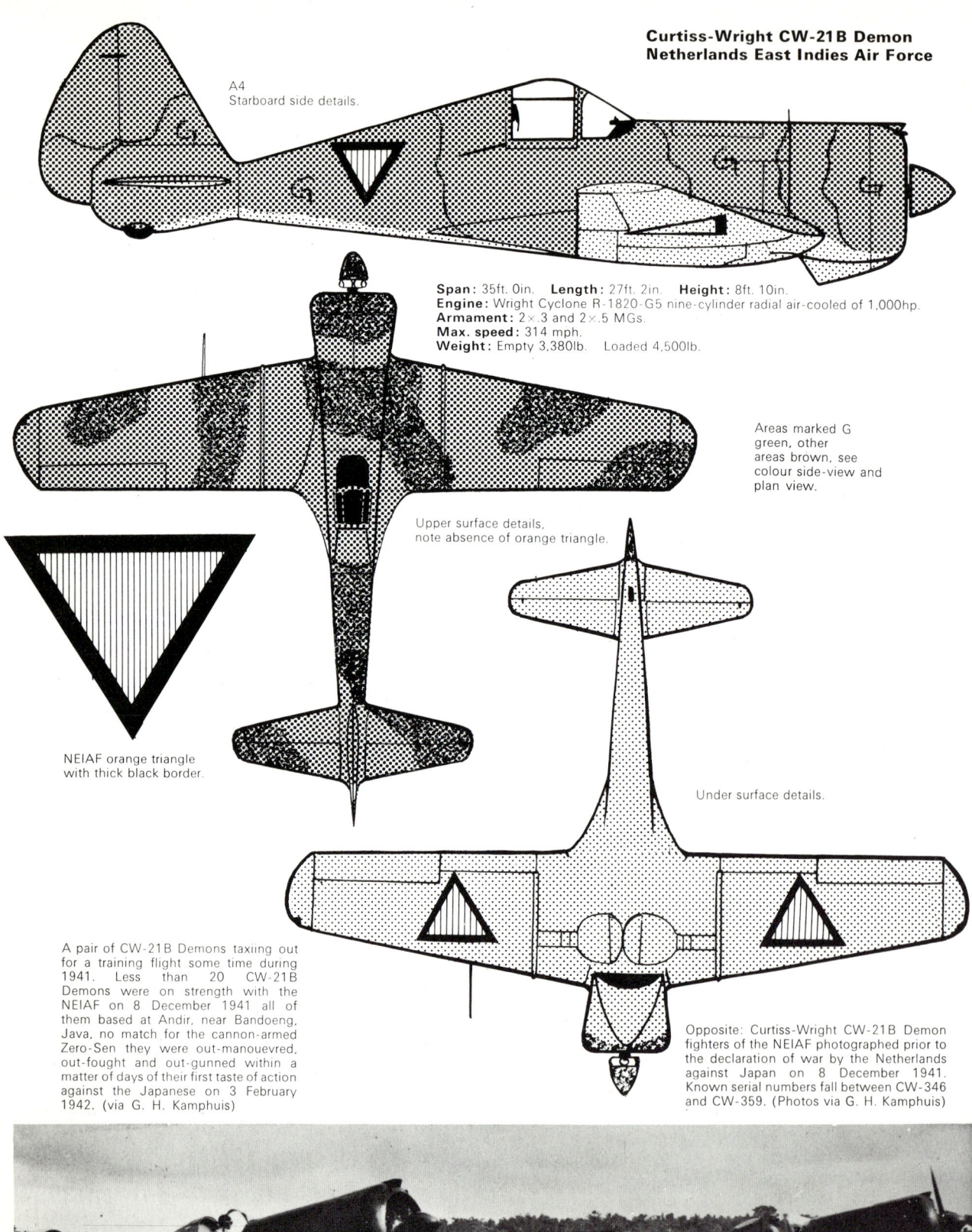

**Curtiss-Wright CW-21B Demon
Netherlands East Indies Air Force**

A4 Starboard side details.

**Span:** 35ft. 0in.  **Length:** 27ft. 2in.  **Height:** 8ft. 10in.
**Engine:** Wright Cyclone R-1820-G5 nine-cylinder radial air-cooled of 1,000hp.
**Armament:** 2×.3 and 2×.5 MGs.
**Max. speed:** 314 mph.
**Weight:** Empty 3,380lb.  Loaded 4,500lb.

Areas marked G green, other areas brown, see colour side-view and plan view.

Upper surface details, note absence of orange triangle.

NEIAF orange triangle with thick black border.

Under surface details.

A pair of CW-21B Demons taxiing out for a training flight some time during 1941. Less than 20 CW-21B Demons were on strength with the NEIAF on 8 December 1941 all of them based at Andir, near Bandoeng, Java, no match for the cannon-armed Zero-Sen they were out-manouevred, out-fought and out-gunned within a matter of days of their first taste of action against the Japanese on 3 February 1942. (via G. H. Kamphuis)

Opposite: Curtiss-Wright CW-21B Demon fighters of the NEIAF photographed prior to the declaration of war by the Netherlands against Japan on 8 December 1941. Known serial numbers fall between CW-346 and CW-359. (Photos via G. H. Kamphuis)

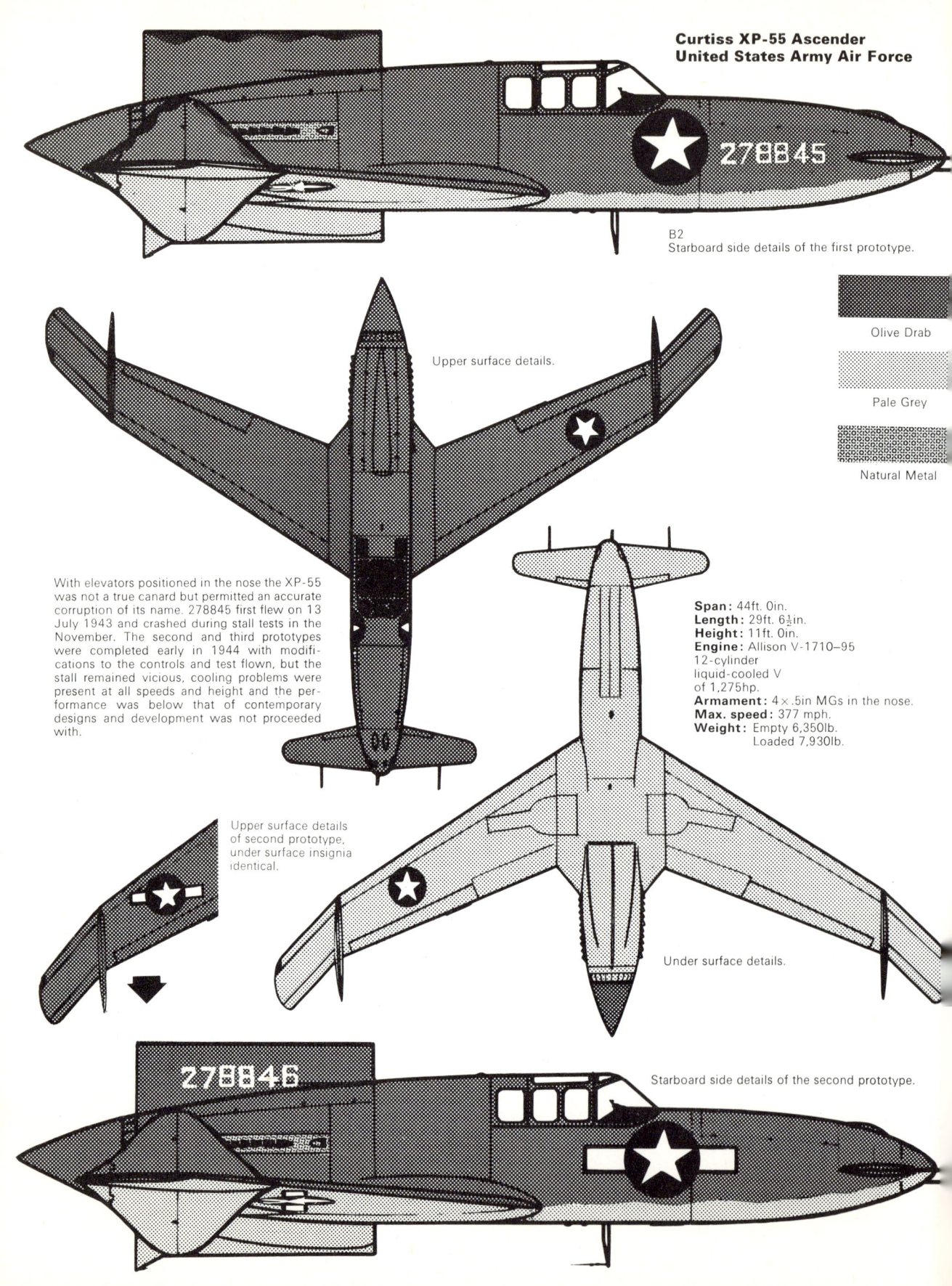

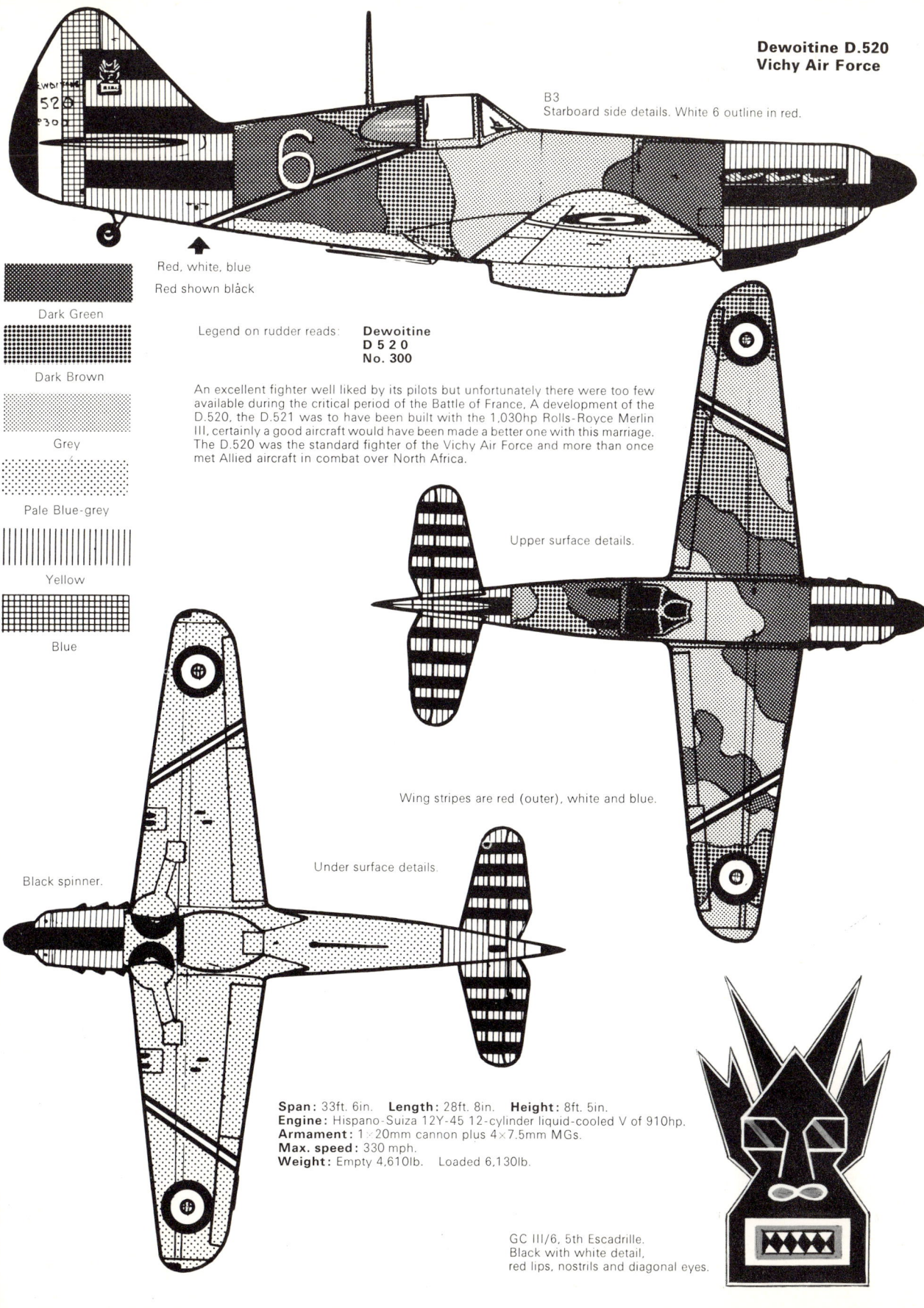

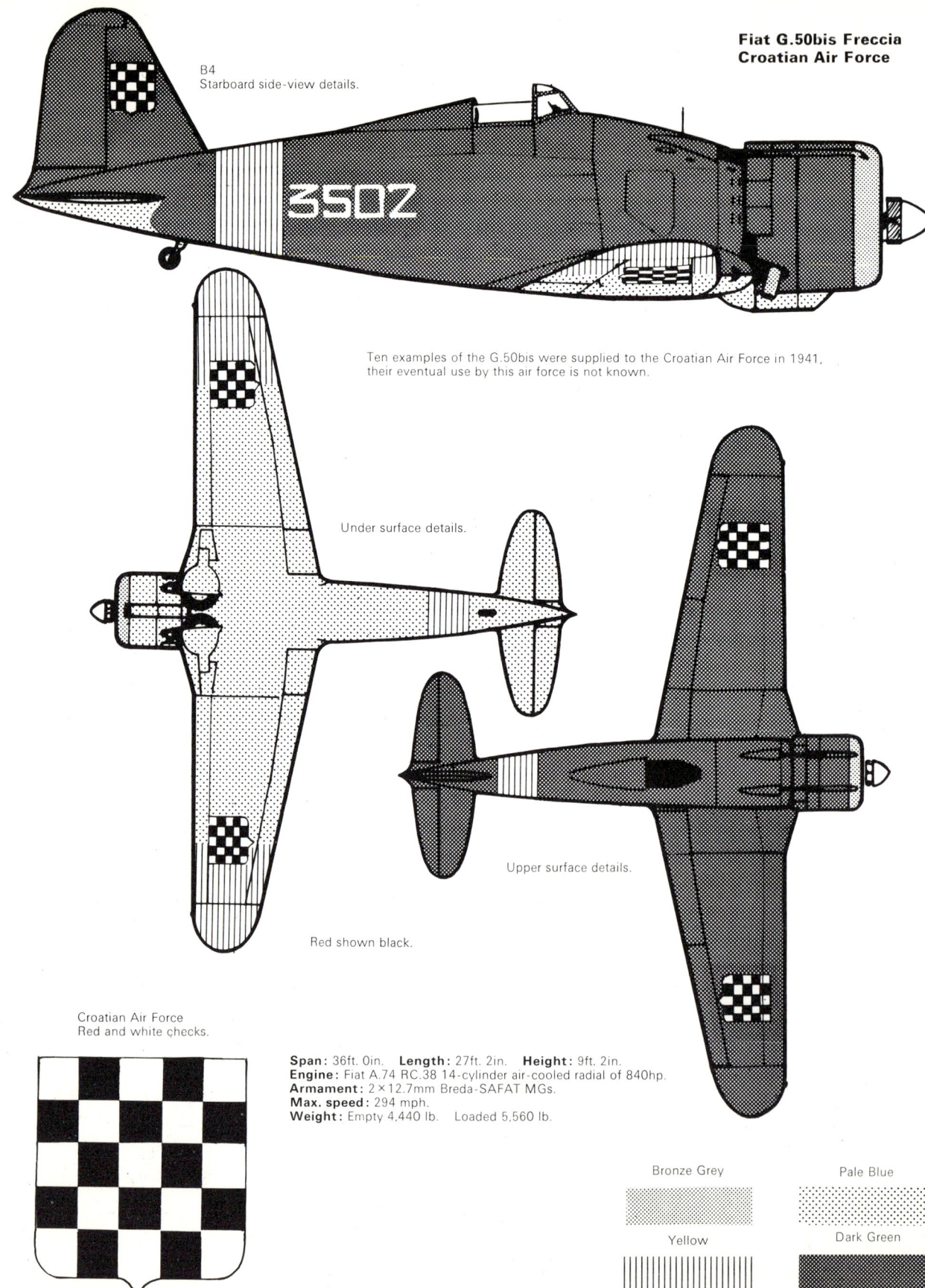

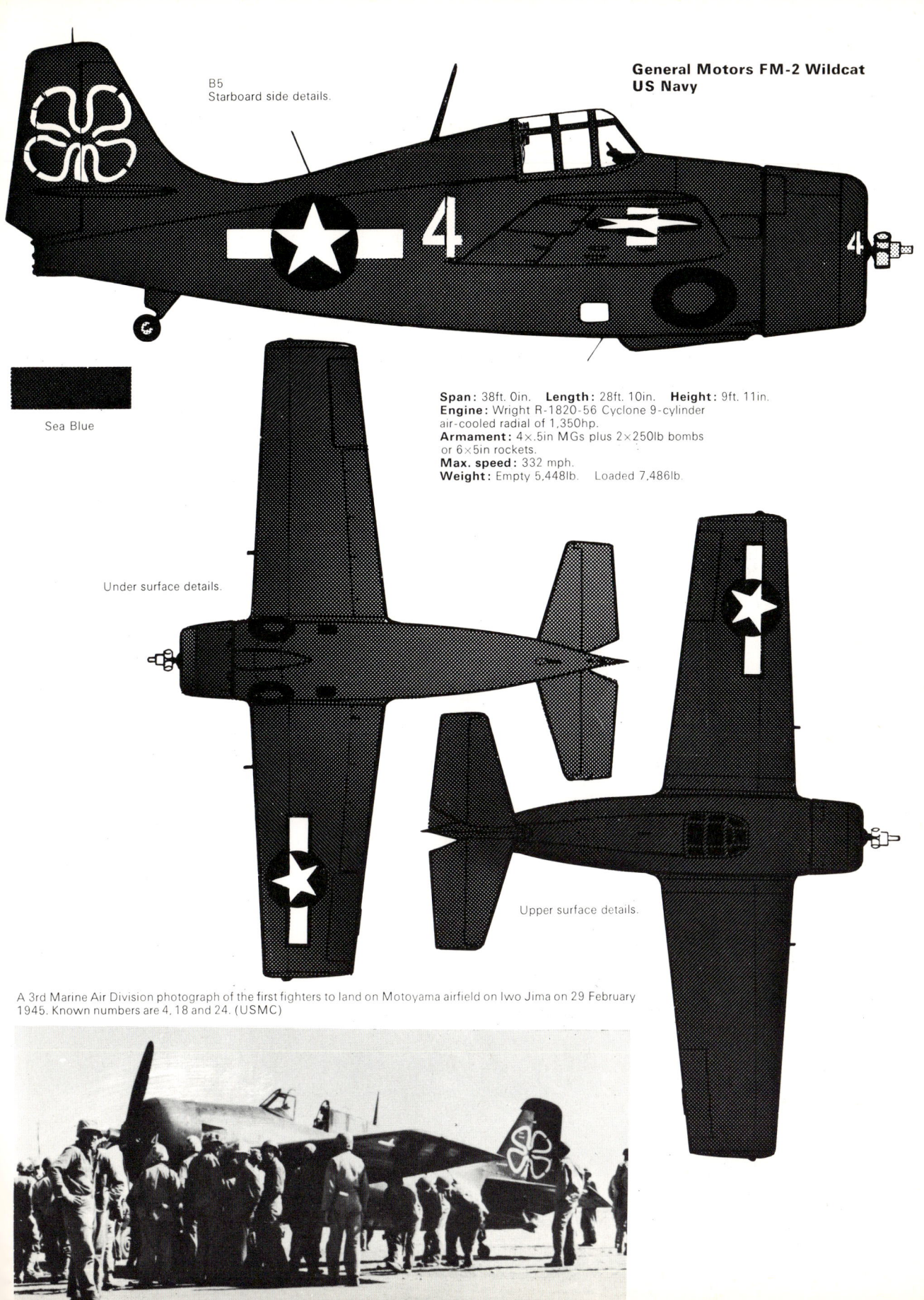

**General Motors FM-2 Wildcat**
**US Navy**

B5 Starboard side details.

Sea Blue

Under surface details.

**Span:** 38ft. 0in.  **Length:** 28ft. 10in.  **Height:** 9ft. 11in.
**Engine:** Wright R-1820-56 Cyclone 9-cylinder air-cooled radial of 1,350hp.
**Armament:** 4×.5in MGs plus 2×250lb bombs or 6×5in rockets.
**Max. speed:** 332 mph.
**Weight:** Empty 5,448lb.  Loaded 7,486lb.

Upper surface details.

A 3rd Marine Air Division photograph of the first fighters to land on Motoyama airfield on Iwo Jima on 29 February 1945. Known numbers are 4, 18 and 24. (USMC)

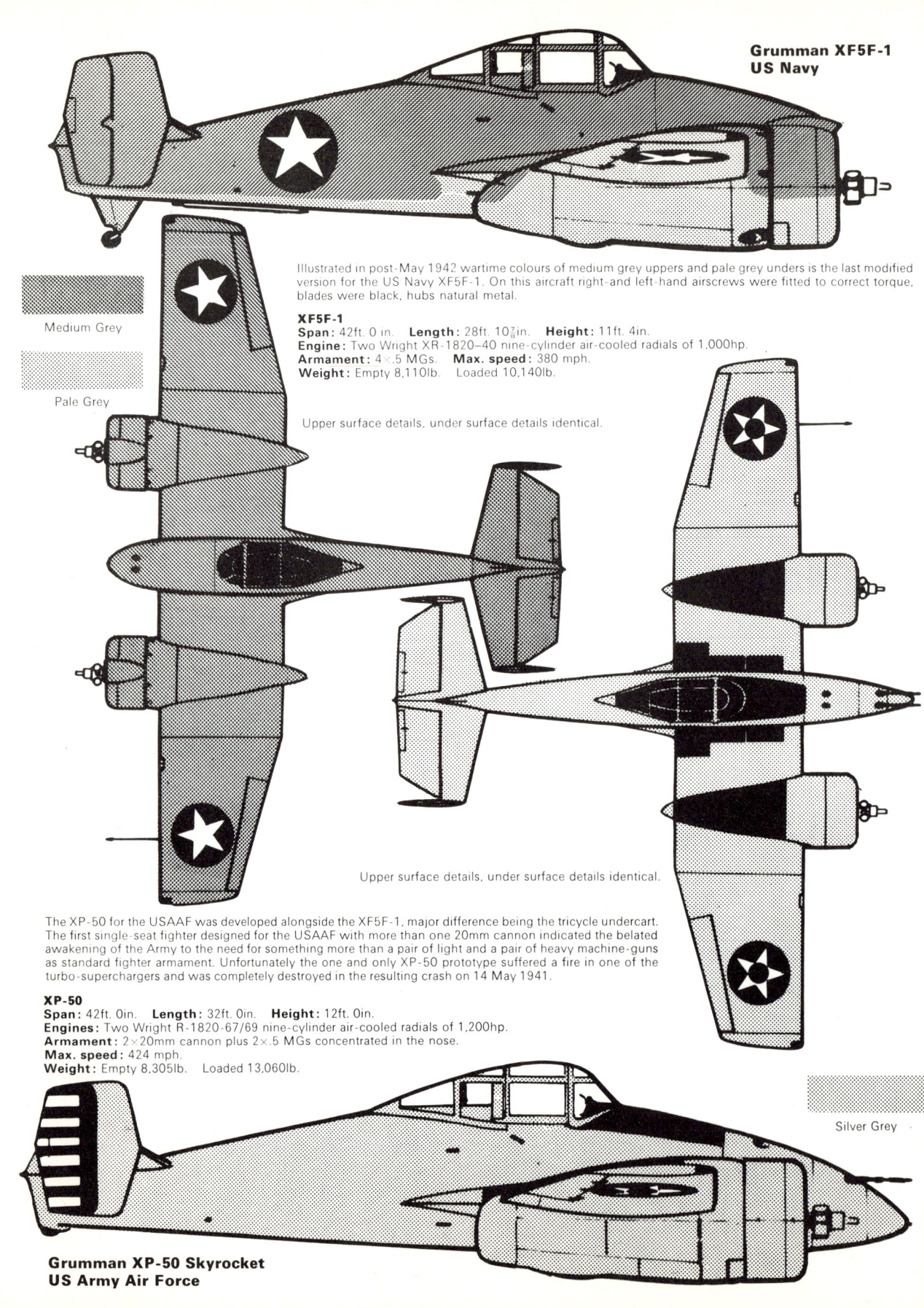

# Grumman XF5F-1 US Navy

Illustrated in post-May 1942 wartime colours of medium grey uppers and pale grey unders is the last modified version for the US Navy XF5F-1. On this aircraft right- and left-hand airscrews were fitted to correct torque, blades were black, hubs natural metal.

**XF5F-1**
**Span:** 42ft. 0 in.  **Length:** 28ft. 10 7/8 in.  **Height:** 11ft. 4in.
**Engine:** Two Wright XR-1820–40 nine-cylinder air-cooled radials of 1,000hp.
**Armament:** 4 × .5 MGs.  **Max. speed:** 380 mph.
**Weight:** Empty 8,110lb.  Loaded 10,140lb.

Upper surface details, under surface details identical.

Medium Grey

Pale Grey

Upper surface details, under surface details identical.

The XP-50 for the USAAF was developed alongside the XF5F-1, major difference being the tricycle undercart. The first single-seat fighter designed for the USAAF with more than one 20mm cannon indicated the belated awakening of the Army to the need for something more than a pair of light and a pair of heavy machine-guns as standard fighter armament. Unfortunately the one and only XP-50 prototype suffered a fire in one of the turbo-superchargers and was completely destroyed in the resulting crash on 14 May 1941.

**XP-50**
**Span:** 42ft. 0in.  **Length:** 32ft. 0in.  **Height:** 12ft. 0in.
**Engines:** Two Wright R-1820-67/69 nine-cylinder air-cooled radials of 1,200hp.
**Armament:** 2 × 20mm cannon plus 2 × .5 MGs concentrated in the nose.
**Max. speed:** 424 mph.
**Weight:** Empty 8,305lb.  Loaded 13,060lb.

Silver Grey

**Grumman XP-50 Skyrocket US Army Air Force**

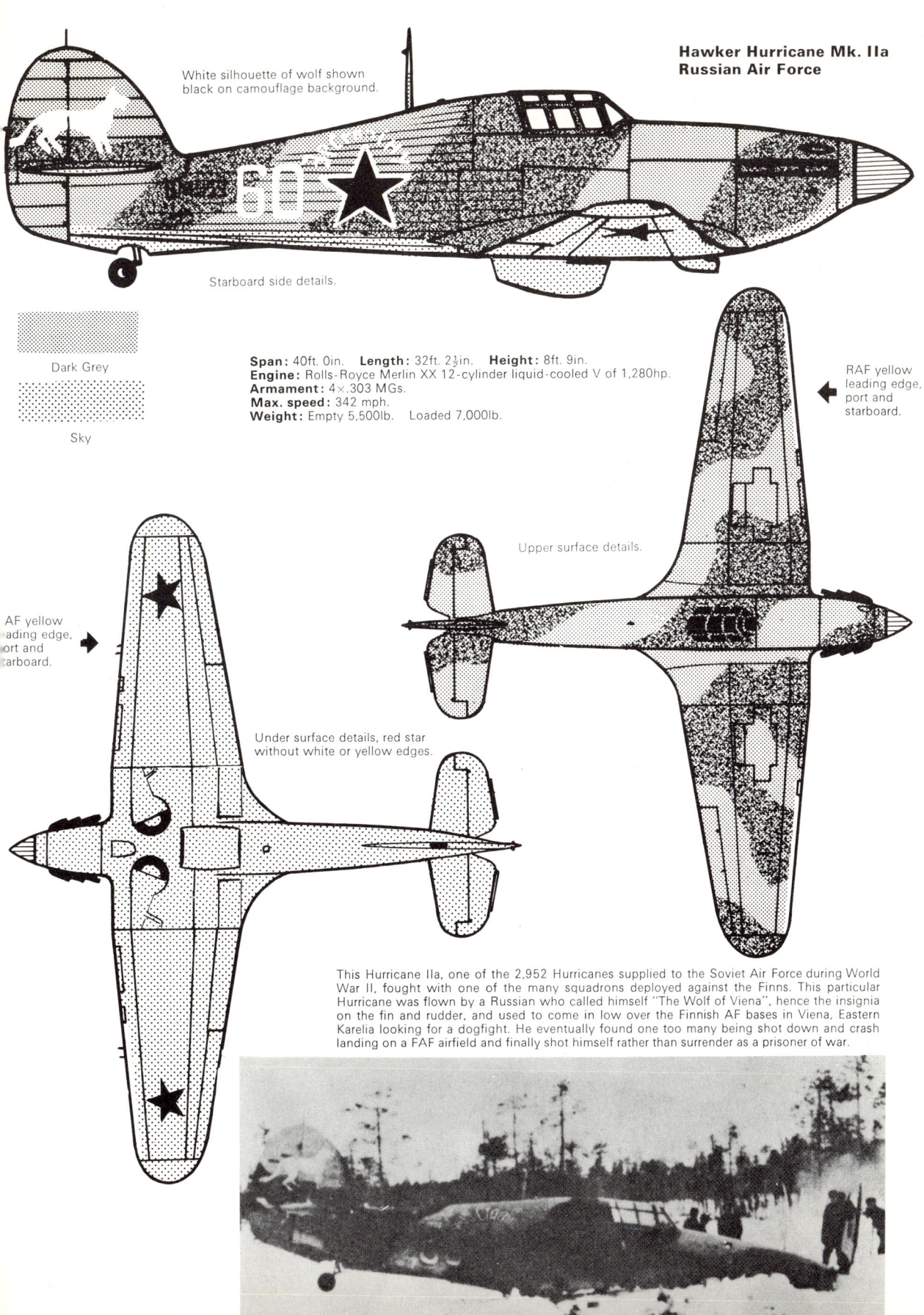

**Hawker Hurricane Mk. IIa Russian Air Force**

White silhouette of wolf shown black on camouflage background.

Starboard side details.

Dark Grey

Sky

Span: 40ft. 0in.　Length: 32ft. 2½in.　Height: 8ft. 9in.
Engine: Rolls-Royce Merlin XX 12-cylinder liquid-cooled V of 1,280hp.
Armament: 4×.303 MGs.
Max. speed: 342 mph.
Weight: Empty 5,500lb.　Loaded 7,000lb.

RAF yellow leading edge, port and starboard.

Upper surface details.

RAF yellow leading edge, port and starboard.

Under surface details, red star without white or yellow edges.

This Hurricane IIa, one of the 2,952 Hurricanes supplied to the Soviet Air Force during World War II, fought with one of the many squadrons deployed against the Finns. This particular Hurricane was flown by a Russian who called himself "The Wolf of Viena", hence the insignia on the fin and rudder, and used to come in low over the Finnish AF bases in Viena, Eastern Karelia looking for a dogfight. He eventually found one too many being shot down and crash landing on a FAF airfield and finally shot himself rather than surrender as a prisoner of war.

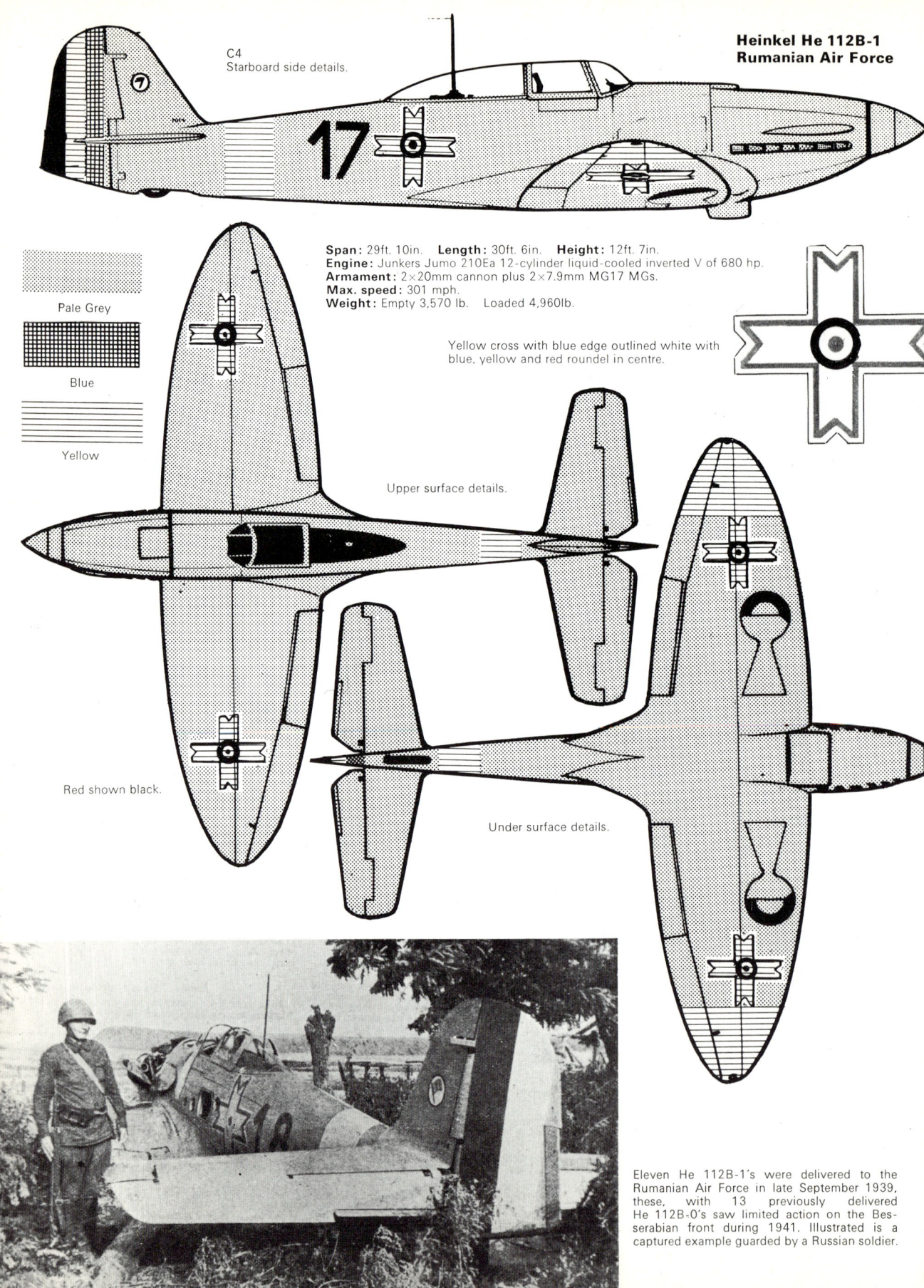

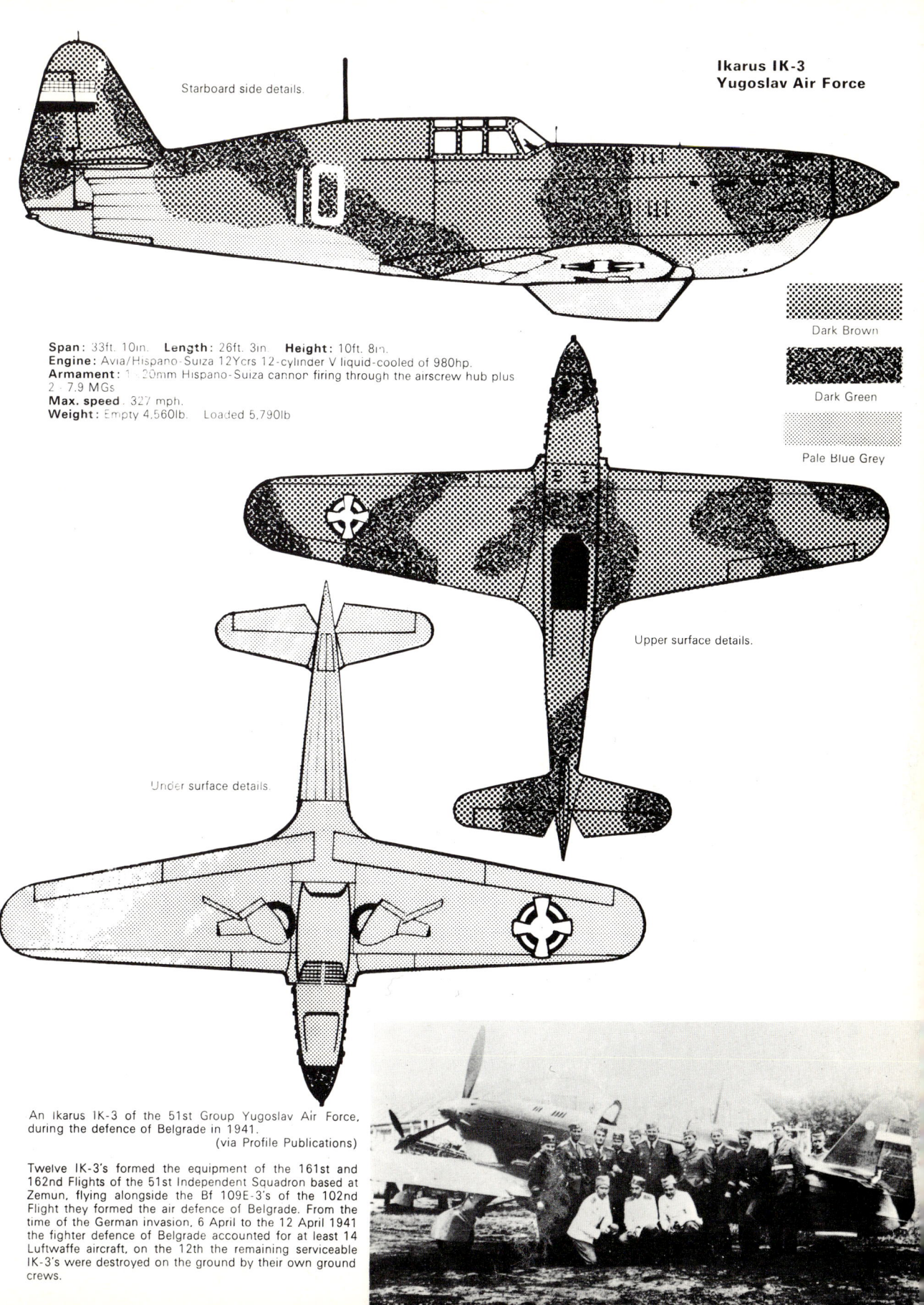

**Ikarus IK-3 Yugoslav Air Force**

Starboard side details.

**Span:** 33ft. 10in. **Length:** 26ft. 3in. **Height:** 10ft. 8in.
**Engine:** Avia/Hispano-Suiza 12Ycrs 12-cylinder V liquid-cooled of 980hp.
**Armament:** 1 - 20mm Hispano-Suiza cannon firing through the airscrew hub plus 2 - 7.9 MGs
**Max. speed:** 327 mph.
**Weight:** Empty 4,560lb. Loaded 5,790lb

Dark Brown

Dark Green

Pale Blue Grey

Upper surface details.

Under surface details.

An Ikarus IK-3 of the 51st Group Yugoslav Air Force, during the defence of Belgrade in 1941.
(via Profile Publications)

Twelve IK-3's formed the equipment of the 161st and 162nd Flights of the 51st Independent Squadron based at Zemun, flying alongside the Bf 109E-3's of the 102nd Flight they formed the air defence of Belgrade. From the time of the German invasion, 6 April to the 12 April 1941 the fighter defence of Belgrade accounted for at least 14 Luftwaffe aircraft, on the 12th the remaining serviceable IK-3's were destroyed on the ground by their own ground crews.

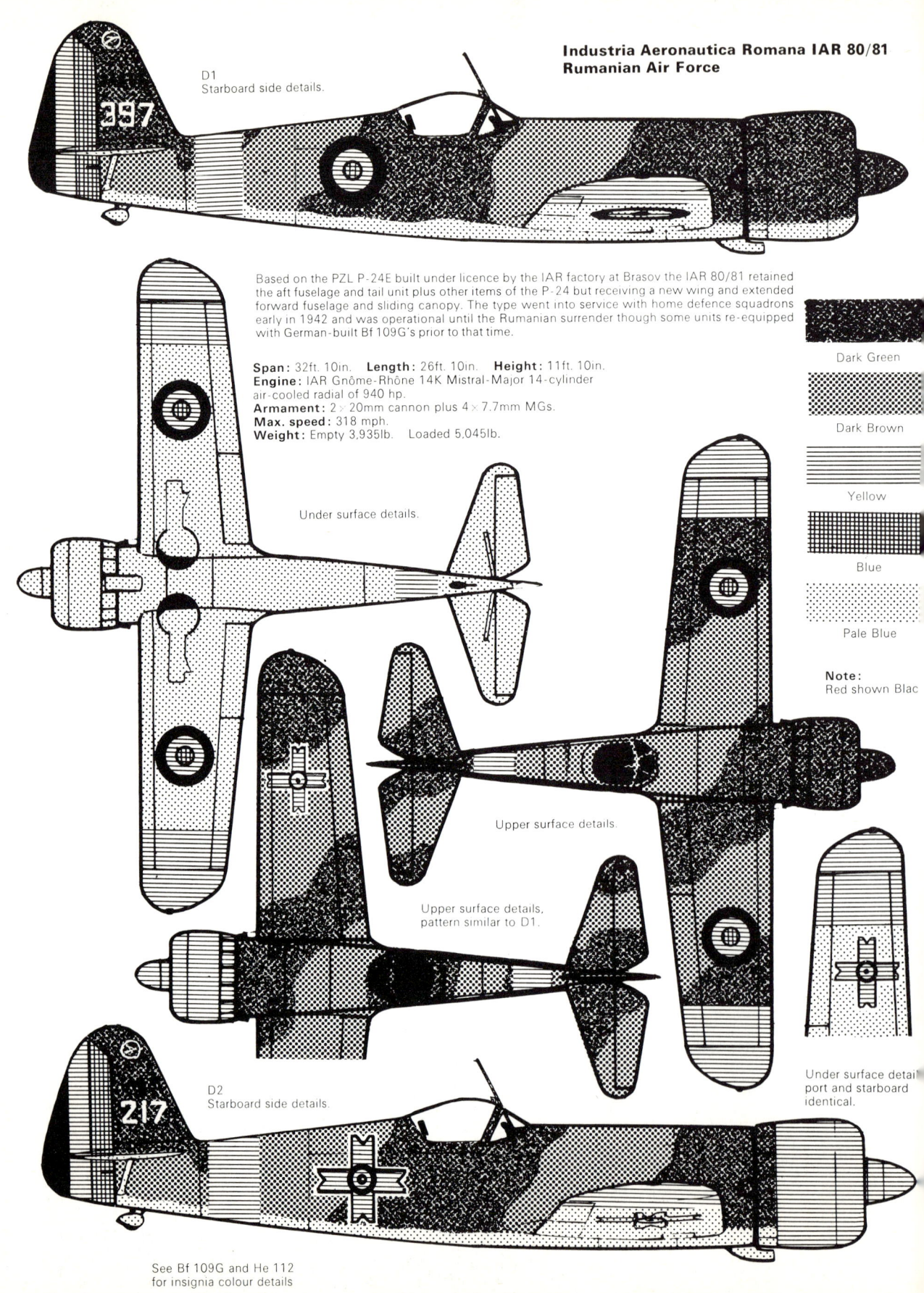

IAR 80 in flight showing clearly the camouflage pattern and the national insignia.

A pair of IAR 80's with the blue, yellow and red roundels in six positions.

Right: Close-up of a bombed-up IAR 81, note the all yellow cowl.

Below: Three-quarter rear shot of a IAR 80, note the fuel markings, position and size of the national insignia. (Photos Moisescu Mihail)

# Industria Aeronautica Romana IAR Bf 109G
## Rumanian Air Force

Starboard side details.

Yellow
Blue
Dark Green
Black Green
Pale Blue.

Rumanian Air Force
Blue, yellow and red. Red shown black.

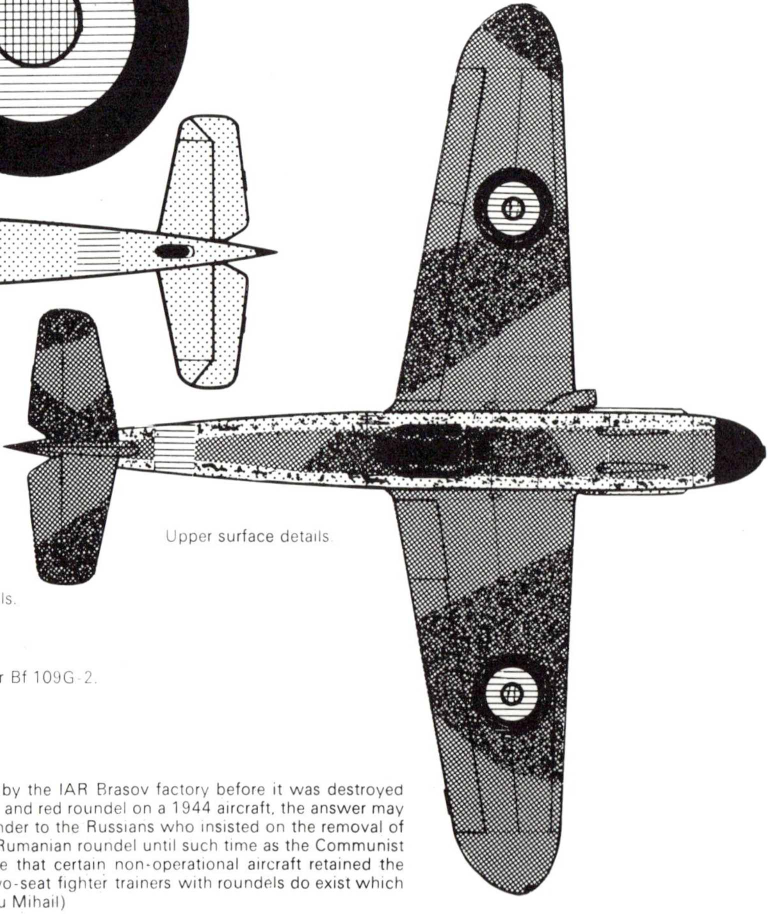

Upper surface details.

Under surface details.

Specification as for Bf 109G-2.

Believed to be one of the 16 or so Bf 109G's completed by the IAR Brasov factory before it was destroyed by Allied air attack in May 1944. Regarding the blue, yellow and red roundel on a 1944 aircraft, the answer may be that the photograph was taken after the Rumanian surrender to the Russians who insisted on the removal of the yellow cross insignia which was replaced by the earlier Rumanian roundel until such time as the Communist inspired present day insignia came into being or it may be that certain non-operational aircraft retained the roundel during the war years as photographs of IAR 80 two-seat fighter trainers with roundels do exist which seem to have been taken prior to the surrender. (via Moisescu Mihail)

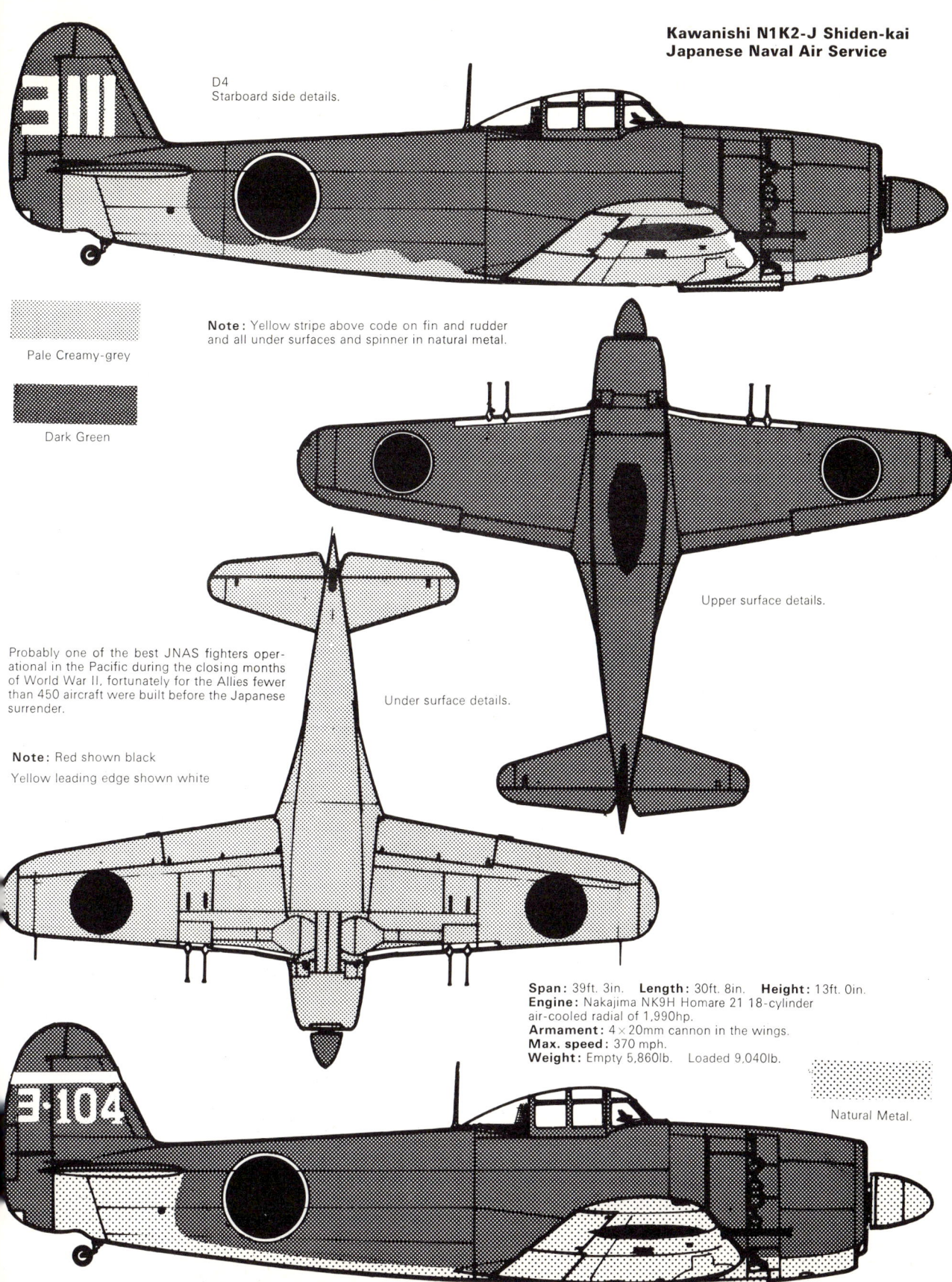

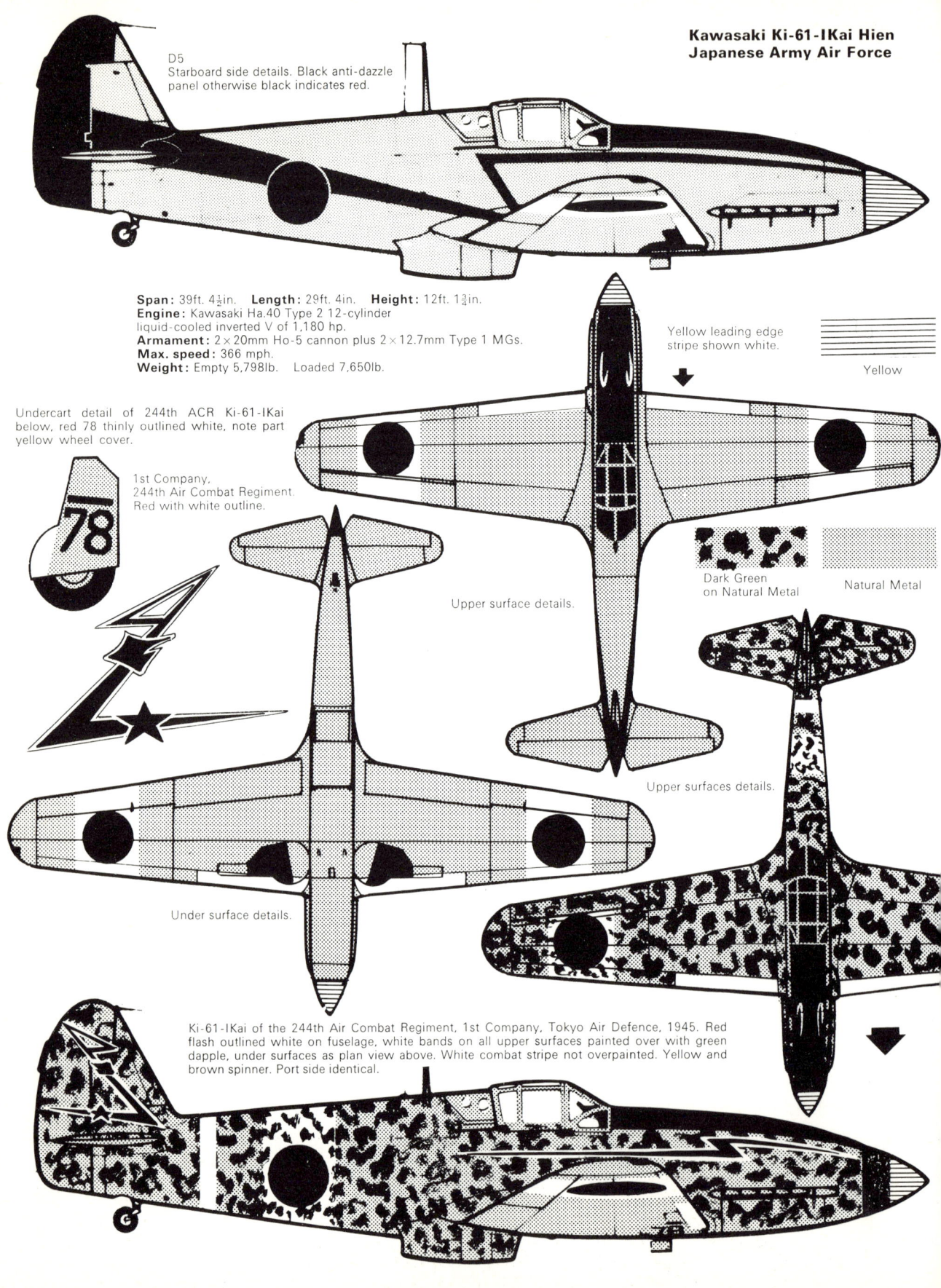

# Lavochkin La5FN
## Czechoslovak Air Force

E1
Starboard side details. Note the thick white surround to the star on fin and rudder and thin red outline to 53 on fuselage.

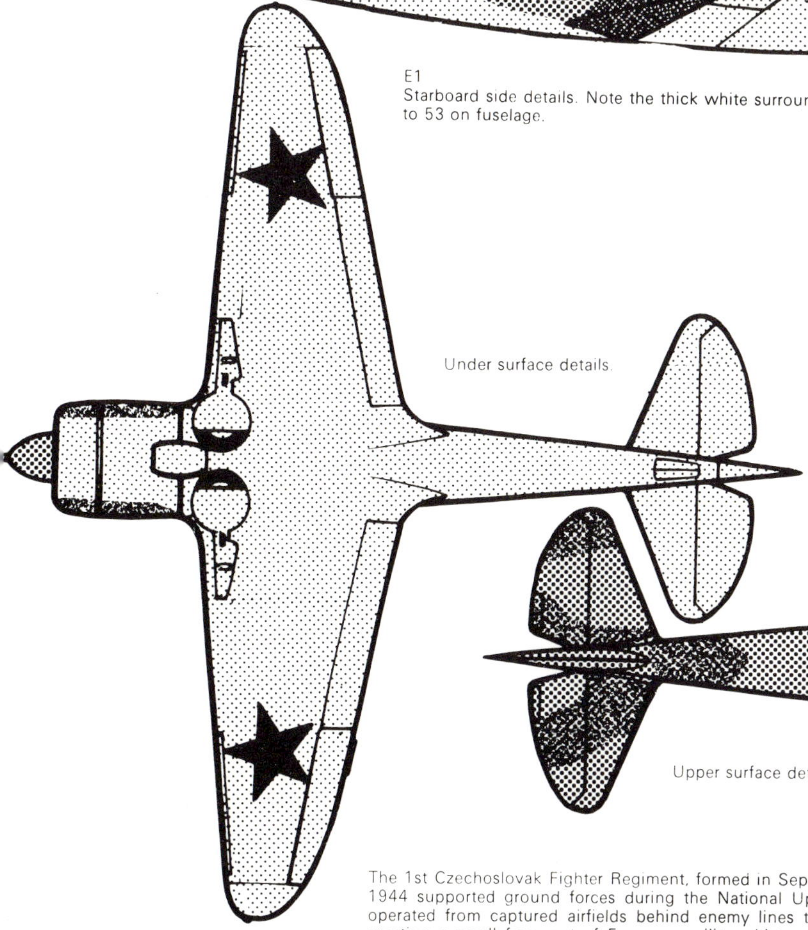

Dark Brown

Pale Blue

Dark Green

Under surface details.

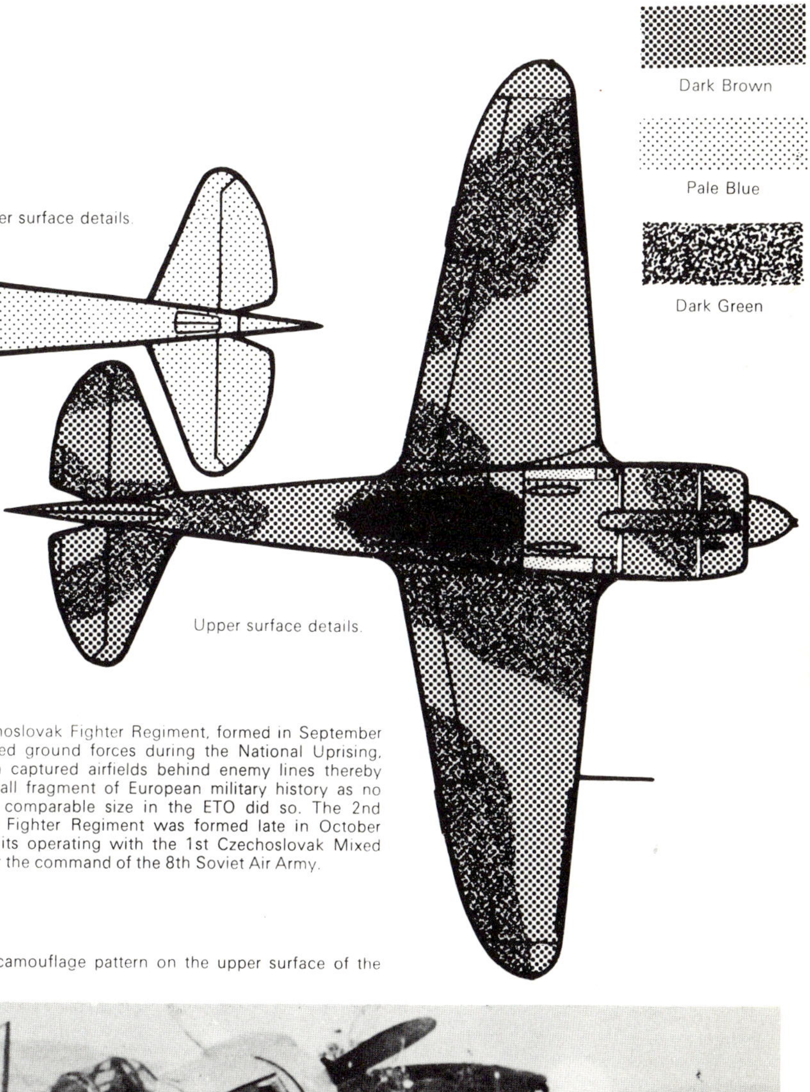

Upper surface details.

The 1st Czechoslovak Fighter Regiment, formed in September 1944 supported ground forces during the National Uprising, operated from captured airfields behind enemy lines thereby creating a small fragment of European military history as no other unit of comparable size in the ETO did so. The 2nd Czechoslovak Fighter Regiment was formed late in October 1944 both units operating with the 1st Czechoslovak Mixed Division under the command of the 8th Soviet Air Army.

Three-quarter rear shot of a La5FN clearly showing the camouflage pattern on the upper surface of the starboard wing, similar scheme to 53 above.

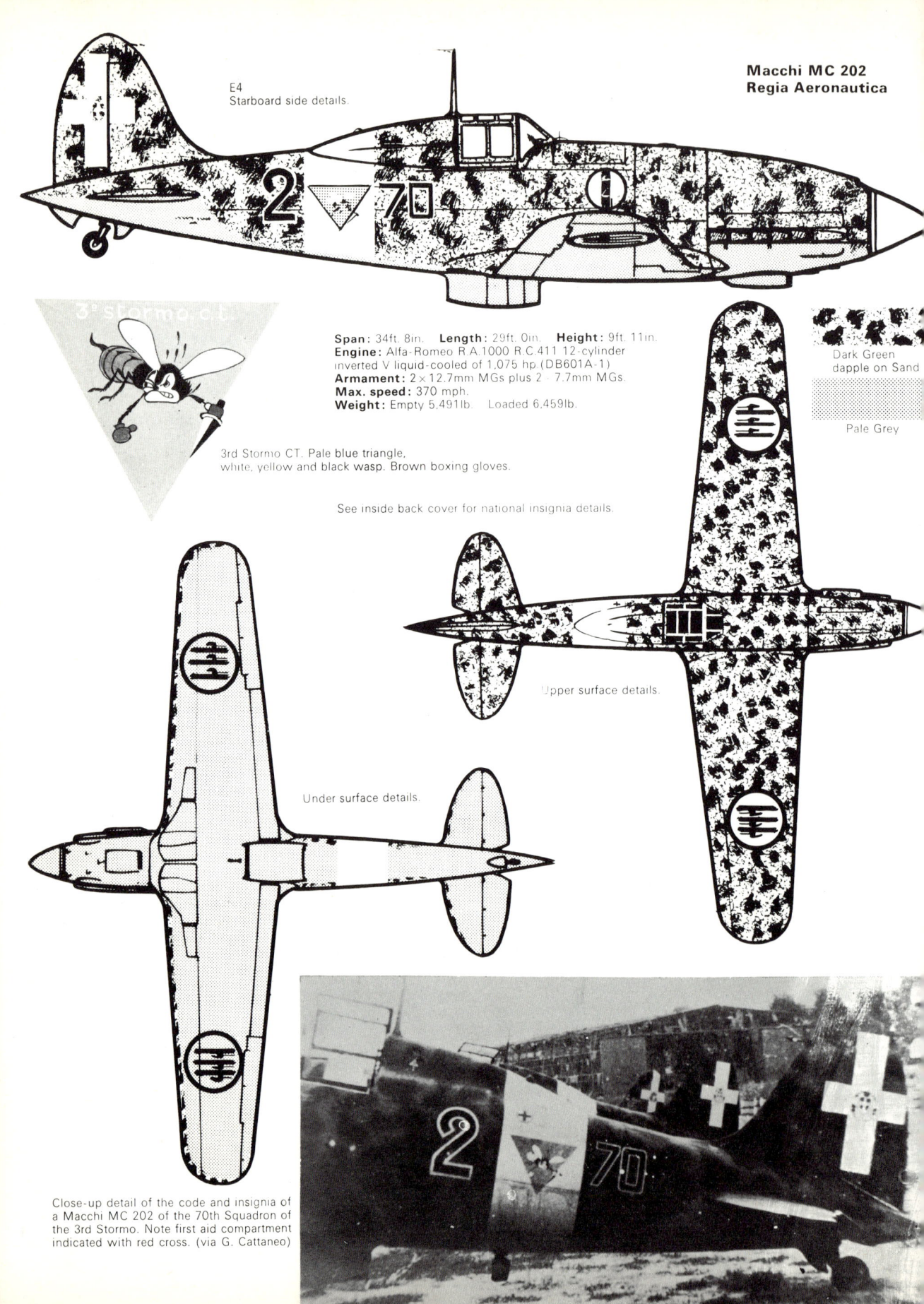

Macchi MC 202
Regia Aeronautica

E4 Starboard side details.

**Span:** 34ft. 8in. **Length:** 29ft. 0in. **Height:** 9ft. 11in.
**Engine:** Alfa-Romeo R.A.1000 R.C.411 12-cylinder inverted V liquid-cooled of 1,075 hp.(DB601A-1)
**Armament:** 2 × 12.7mm MGs plus 2 – 7.7mm MGs.
**Max. speed:** 370 mph.
**Weight:** Empty 5,491lb. Loaded 6,459lb.

3rd Stormo CT. Pale blue triangle, white, yellow and black wasp. Brown boxing gloves.

See inside back cover for national insignia details.

Dark Green dapple on Sand

Pale Grey

Upper surface details.

Under surface details.

Close-up detail of the code and insignia of a Macchi MC 202 of the 70th Squadron of the 3rd Stormo. Note first aid compartment indicated with red cross. (via G. Cattaneo)

A

1 Avia B-135, Bulgarian Air Force. 1941.

2 Caudron C.714, Groupe de Chasse Polonaise de Varsovie I/145. June 1940

3 Caudron C.714, Groupe de Chasse Polonaise I/145. June 1940.

4 Curtiss Wright CW-21B Demon, Netherlands East Indies Air Force. 1940–41.

5 Curtiss Hawk 75A-7, Netherlands East Indies Air Force. 1940–41.

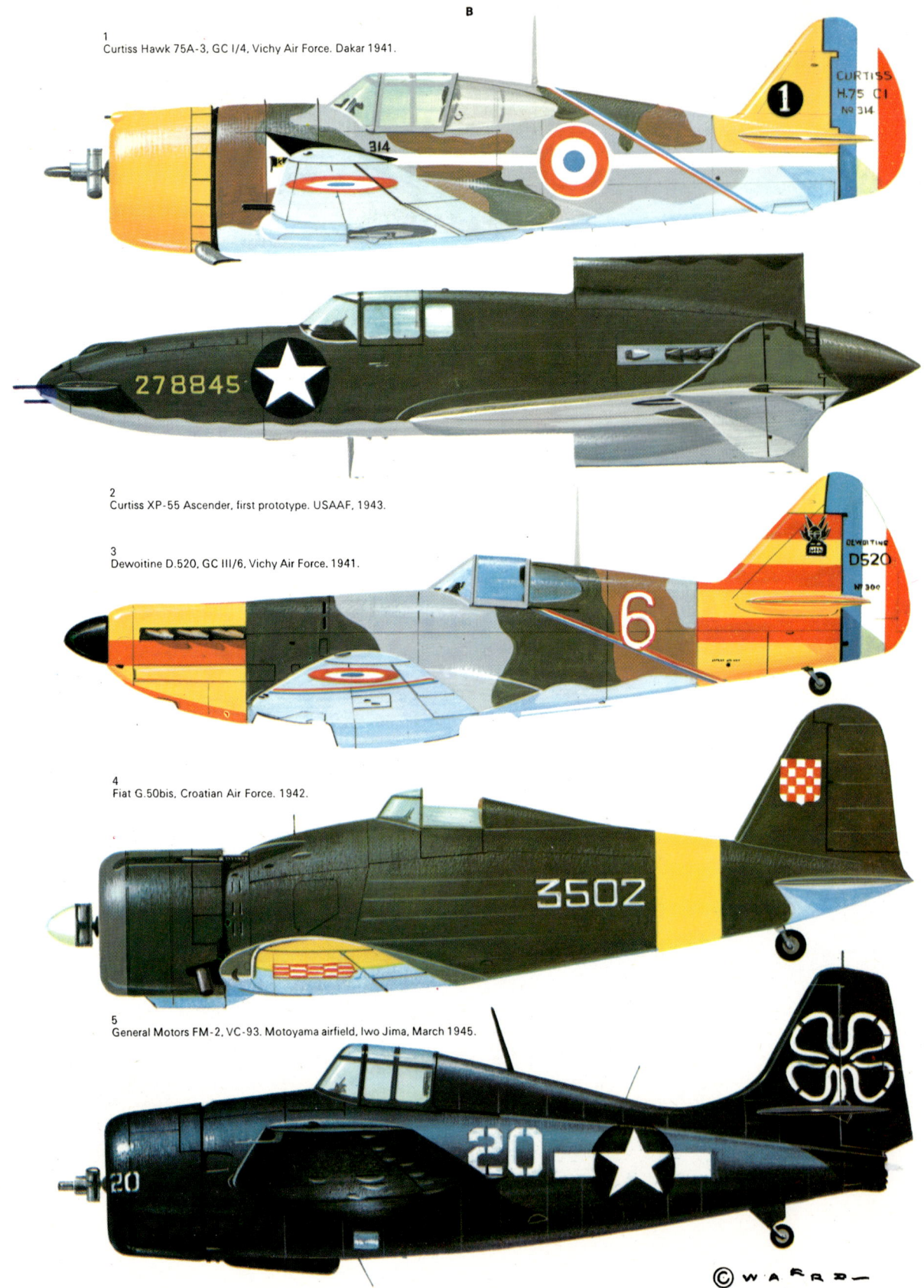

1 Curtiss Hawk 75A-3, GC I/4, Vichy Air Force. Dakar 1941.

2 Curtiss XP-55 Ascender, first prototype. USAAF, 1943.

3 Dewoitine D.520, GC III/6, Vichy Air Force. 1941.

4 Fiat G.50bis, Croatian Air Force. 1942.

5 General Motors FM-2, VC-93. Motoyama airfield, Iwo Jima, March 1945.

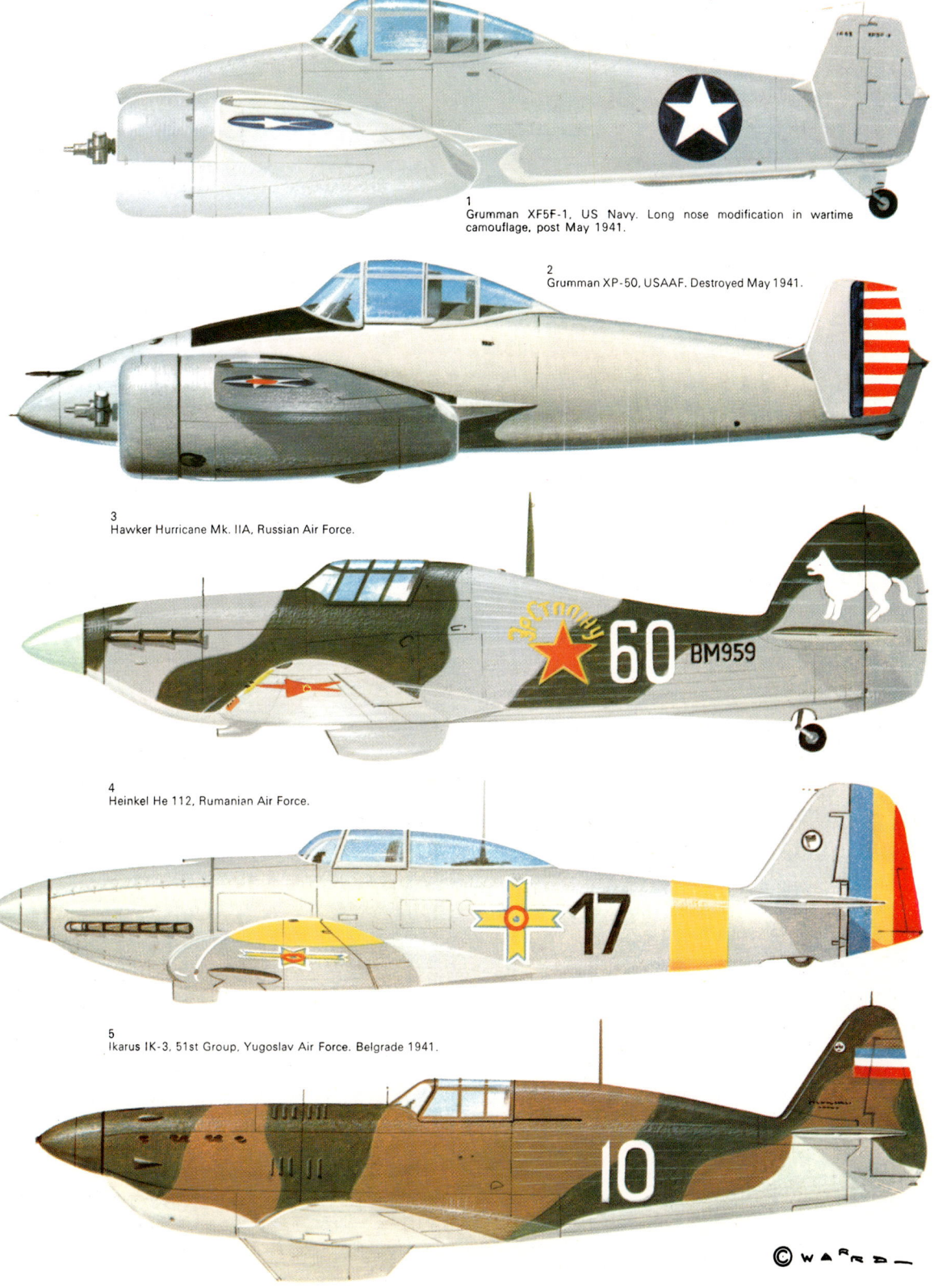

1 Grumman XF5F-1, US Navy. Long nose modification in wartime camouflage, post May 1941.

2 Grumman XP-50, USAAF. Destroyed May 1941.

3 Hawker Hurricane Mk. IIA, Russian Air Force.

4 Heinkel He 112, Rumanian Air Force.

5 Ikarus IK-3, 51st Group, Yugoslav Air Force. Belgrade 1941.

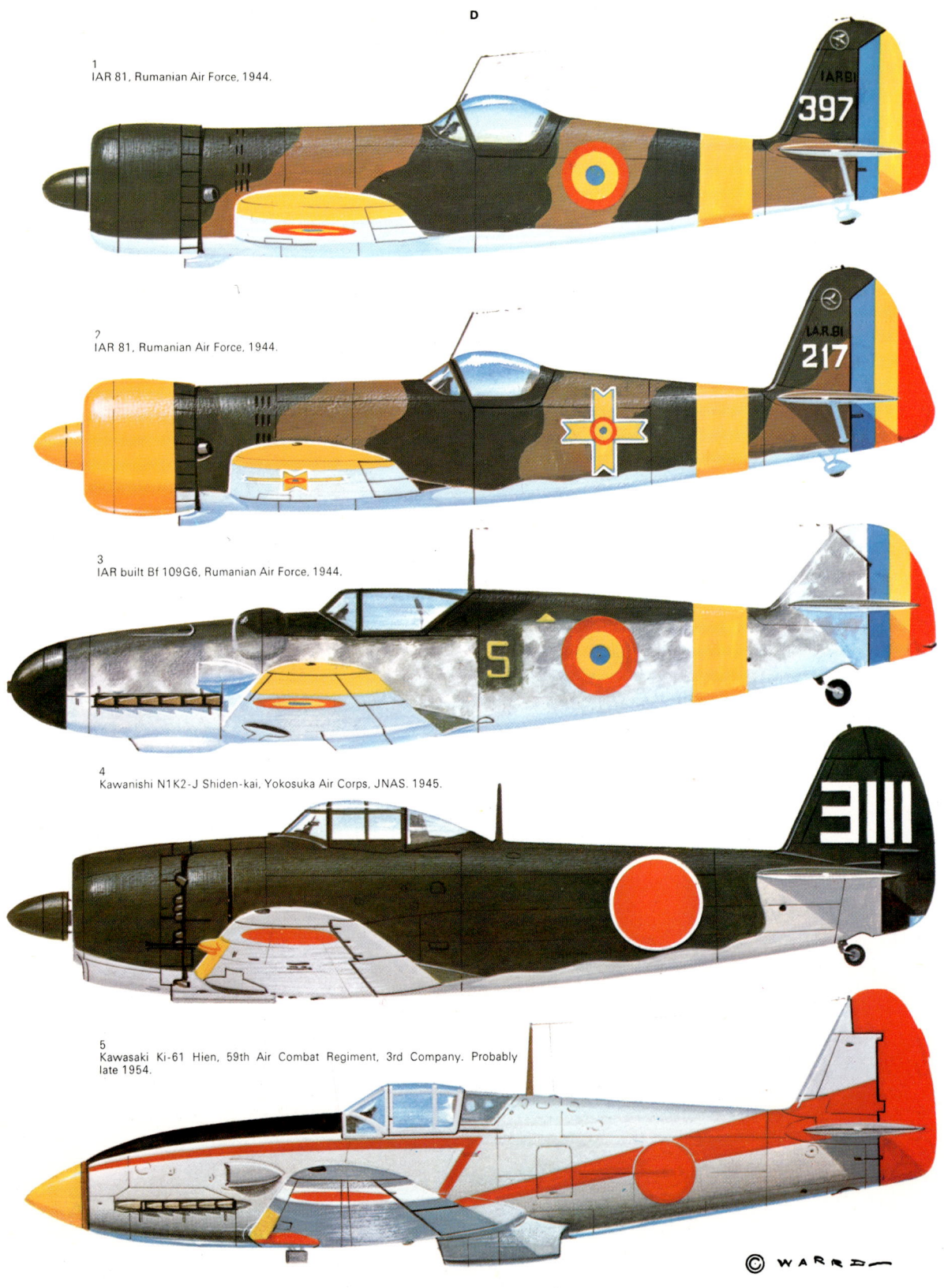

D

1 IAR 81, Rumanian Air Force, 1944.

2 IAR 81, Rumanian Air Force, 1944.

3 IAR built Bf 109G6, Rumanian Air Force, 1944.

4 Kawanishi N1K2-J Shiden-kai, Yokosuka Air Corps, JNAS. 1945.

5 Kawasaki Ki-61 Hien, 59th Air Combat Regiment, 3rd Company. Probably late 1954.

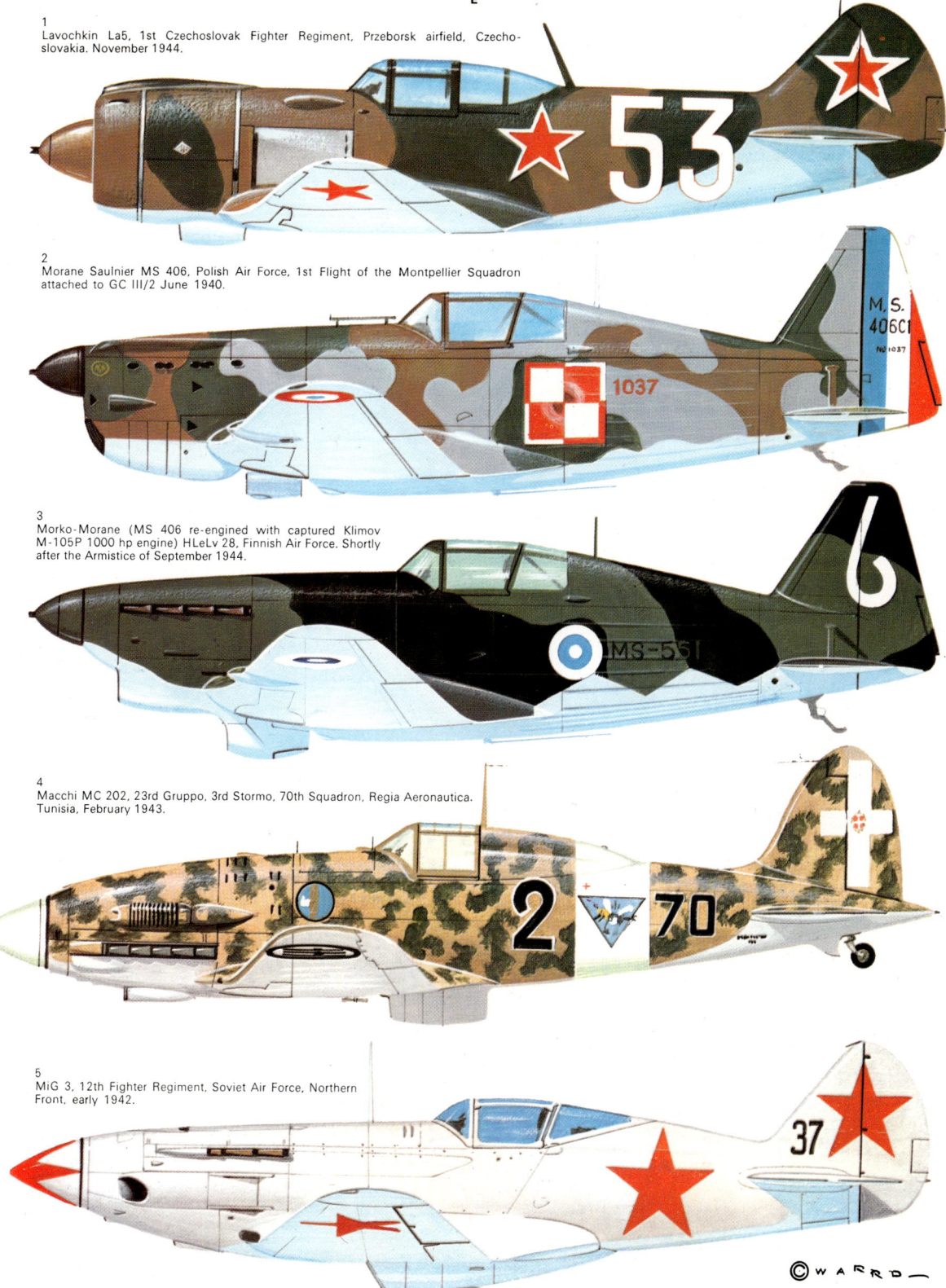

1
Lavochkin La5, 1st Czechoslovak Fighter Regiment, Przeborsk airfield, Czechoslovakia. November 1944.

2
Morane Saulnier MS 406, Polish Air Force, 1st Flight of the Montpellier Squadron attached to GC III/2 June 1940.

3
Morko-Morane (MS 406 re-engined with captured Klimov M-105P 1000 hp engine) HLeLv 28, Finnish Air Force. Shortly after the Armistice of September 1944.

4
Macchi MC 202, 23rd Gruppo, 3rd Stormo, 70th Squadron, Regia Aeronautica. Tunisia, February 1943.

5
MiG 3, 12th Fighter Regiment, Soviet Air Force, Northern Front, early 1942.

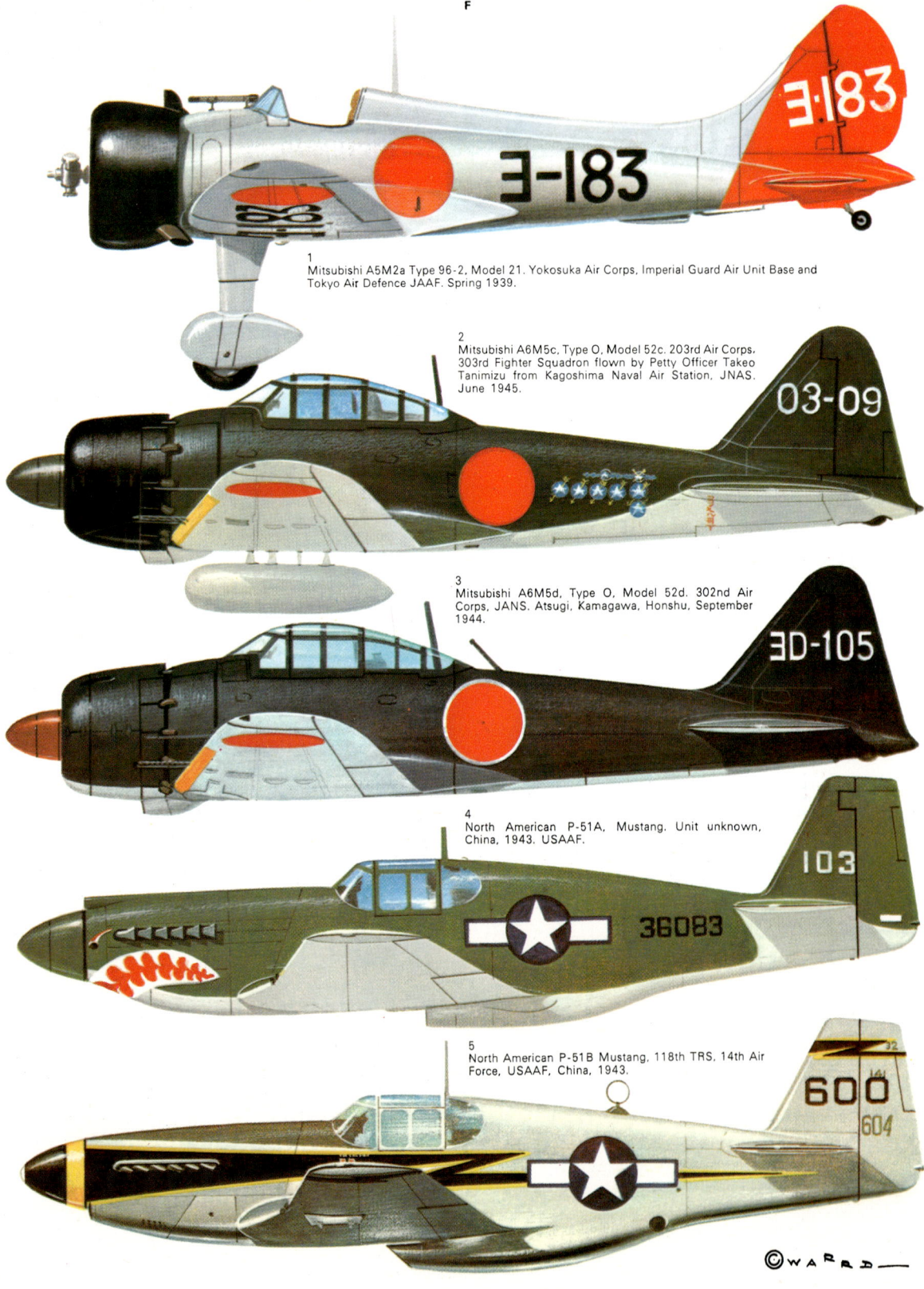

1 Mitsubishi A5M2a Type 96-2, Model 21. Yokosuka Air Corps, Imperial Guard Air Unit Base and Tokyo Air Defence JAAF. Spring 1939.

2 Mitsubishi A6M5c, Type O, Model 52c. 203rd Air Corps, 303rd Fighter Squadron flown by Petty Officer Takeo Tanimizu from Kagoshima Naval Air Station, JNAS. June 1945.

3 Mitsubishi A6M5d, Type O, Model 52d. 302nd Air Corps, JANS. Atsugi, Kamagawa, Honshu, September 1944.

4 North American P-51A, Mustang. Unit unknown, China, 1943. USAAF.

5 North American P-51B Mustang, 118th TRS, 14th Air Force, USAAF, China, 1943.

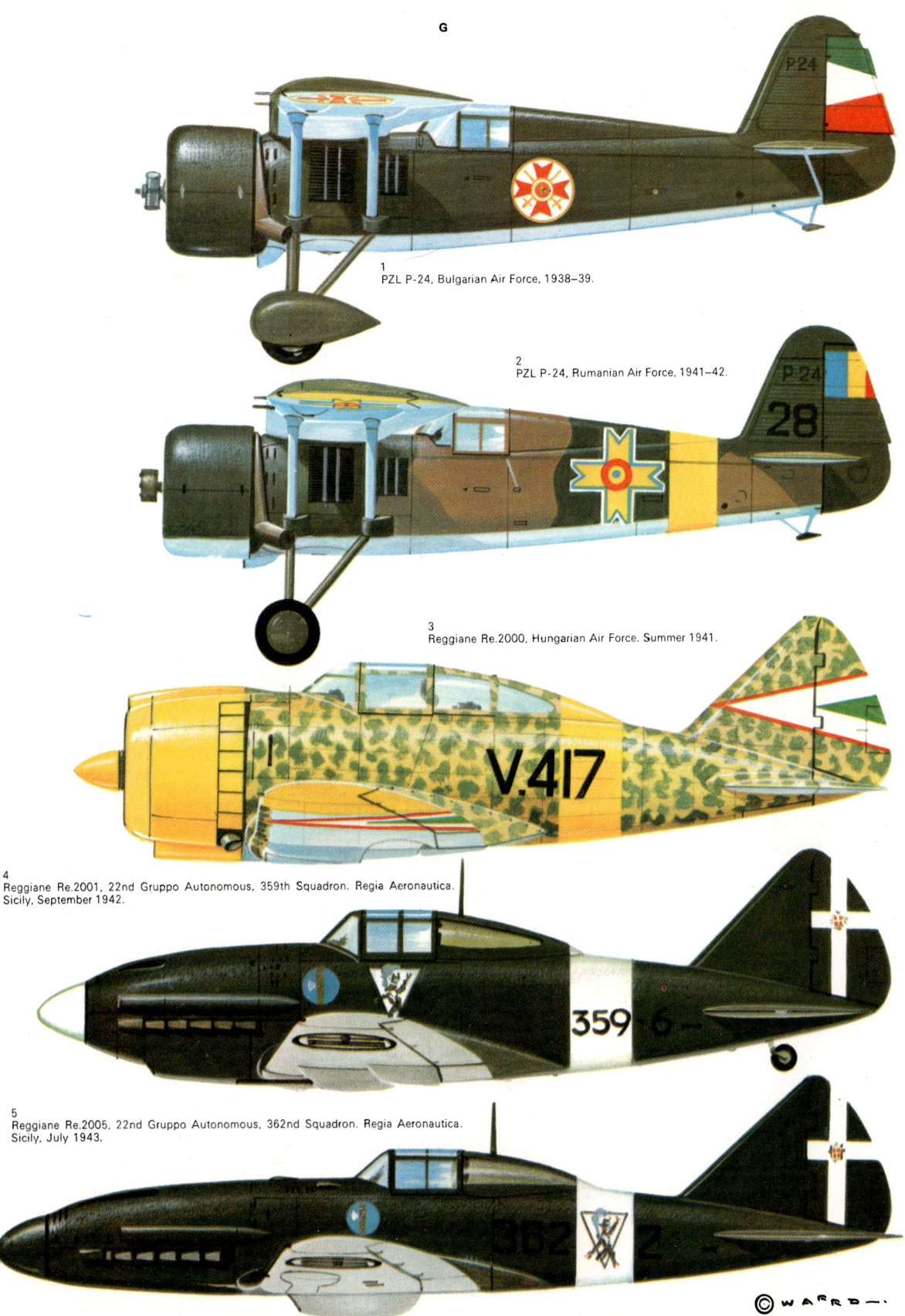

G

1
PZL P-24, Bulgarian Air Force, 1938–39.

2
PZL P-24, Rumanian Air Force, 1941–42.

3
Reggiane Re.2000, Hungarian Air Force. Summer 1941.

4
Reggiane Re.2001, 22nd Gruppo Autonomous, 359th Squadron. Regia Aeronautica. Sicily, September 1942.

5
Reggiane Re.2005, 22nd Gruppo Autonomous, 362nd Squadron. Regia Aeronautica. Sicily, July 1943.

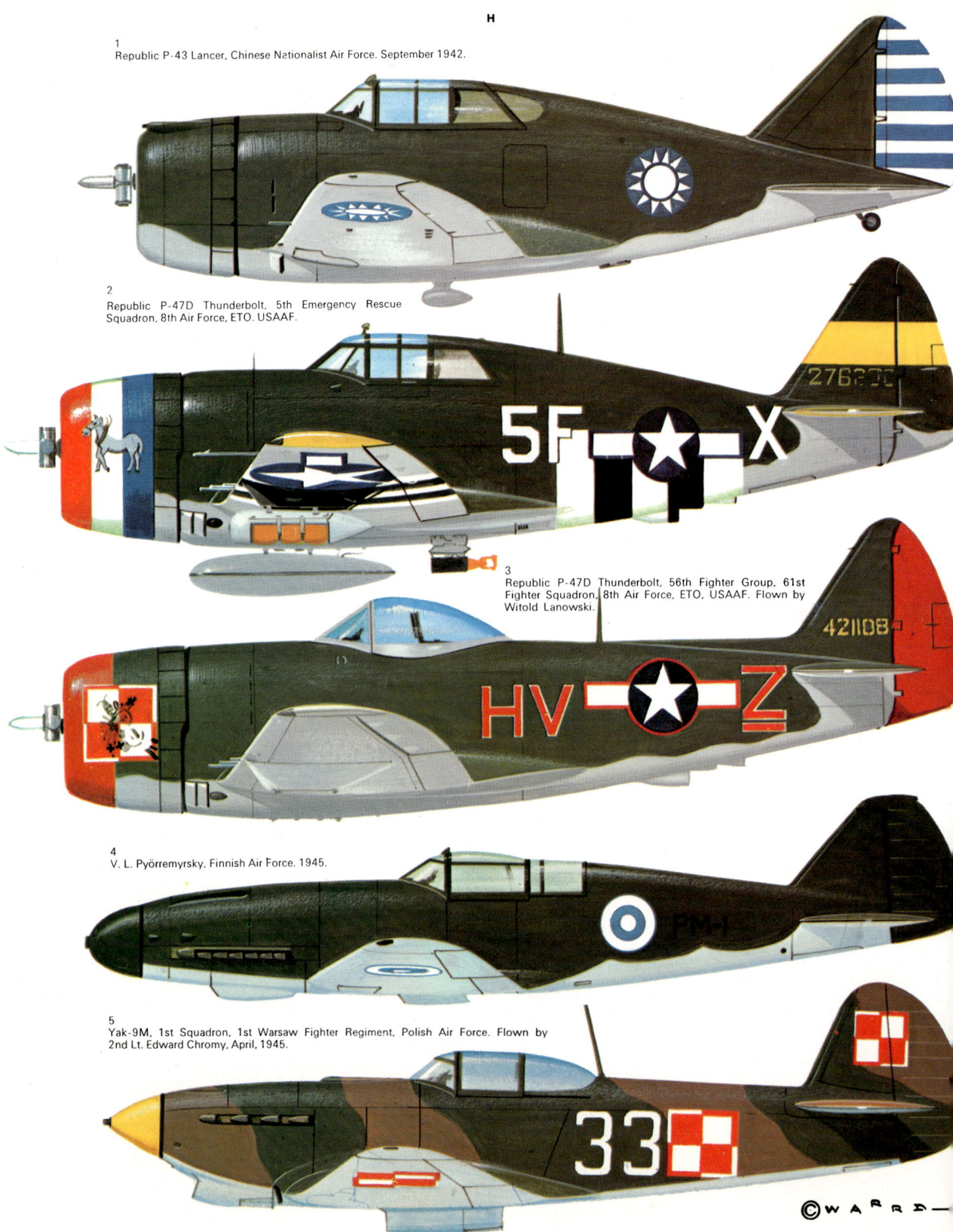

H

1 Republic P-43 Lancer, Chinese Nationalist Air Force. September 1942.

2 Republic P-47D Thunderbolt, 5th Emergency Rescue Squadron, 8th Air Force, ETO. USAAF.

3 Republic P-47D Thunderbolt, 56th Fighter Group, 61st Fighter Squadron, 8th Air Force, ETO, USAAF. Flown by Witold Lanowski.

4 V. L. Pyörremyrsky, Finnish Air Force. 1945.

5 Yak-9M, 1st Squadron, 1st Warsaw Fighter Regiment, Polish Air Force. Flown by 2nd Lt. Edward Chromy, April, 1945.

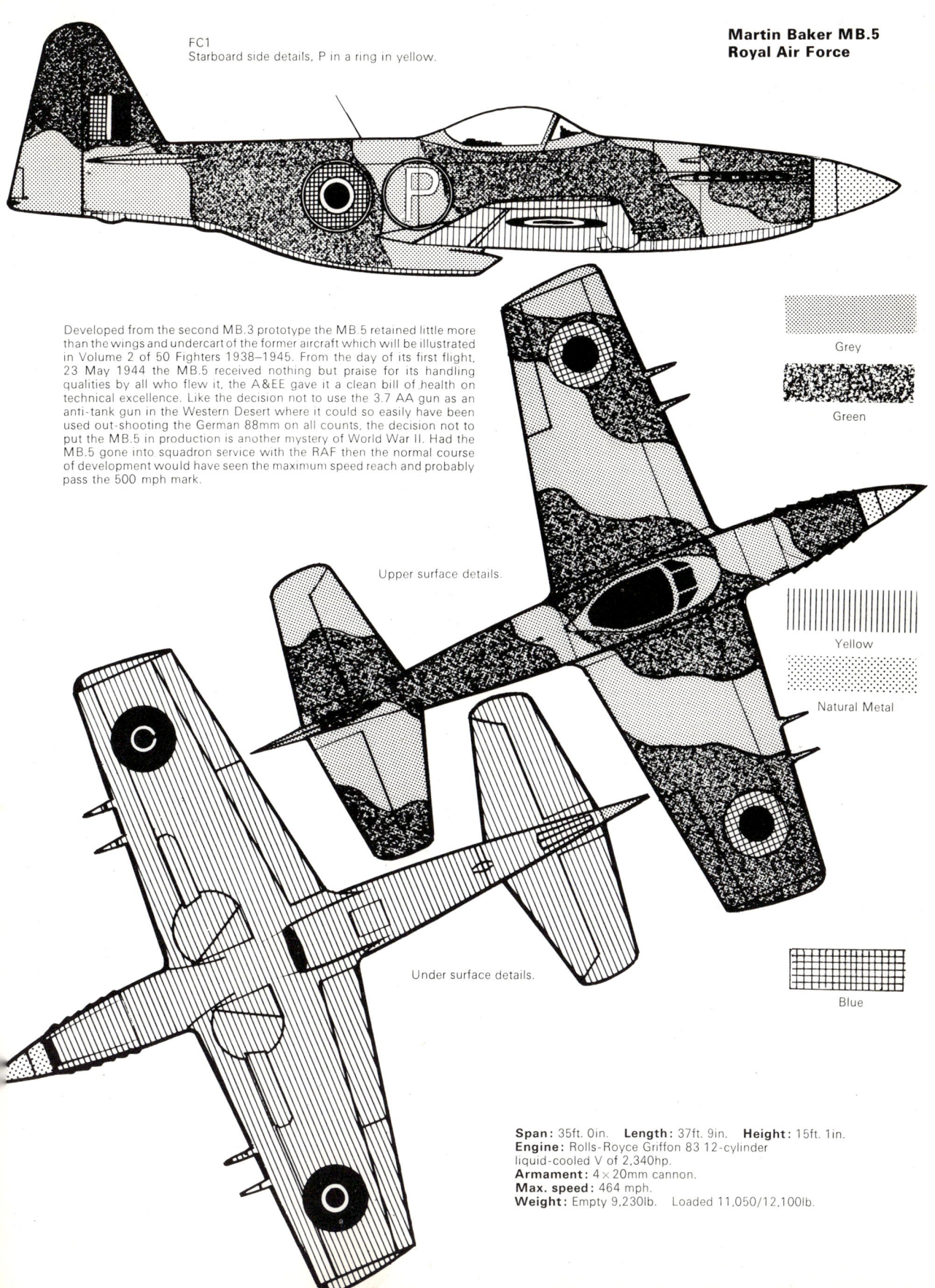

**Martin Baker MB.5**
**Royal Air Force**

FC1
Starboard side details, P in a ring in yellow.

Developed from the second MB.3 prototype the MB.5 retained little more than the wings and undercart of the former aircraft which will be illustrated in Volume 2 of 50 Fighters 1938–1945. From the day of its first flight, 23 May 1944 the MB.5 received nothing but praise for its handling qualities by all who flew it, the A&EE gave it a clean bill of health on technical excellence. Like the decision not to use the 3.7 AA gun as an anti-tank gun in the Western Desert where it could so easily have been used out-shooting the German 88mm on all counts, the decision not to put the MB.5 in production is another mystery of World War II. Had the MB.5 gone into squadron service with the RAF then the normal course of development would have seen the maximum speed reach and probably pass the 500 mph mark.

Upper surface details.

Under surface details.

Grey
Green
Yellow
Natural Metal
Blue

**Span:** 35ft. 0in. **Length:** 37ft. 9in. **Height:** 15ft. 1in.
**Engine:** Rolls-Royce Griffon 83 12-cylinder liquid-cooled V of 2,340hp.
**Armament:** 4 × 20mm cannon.
**Max. speed:** 464 mph.
**Weight:** Empty 9,230lb.   Loaded 11,050/12,100lb.

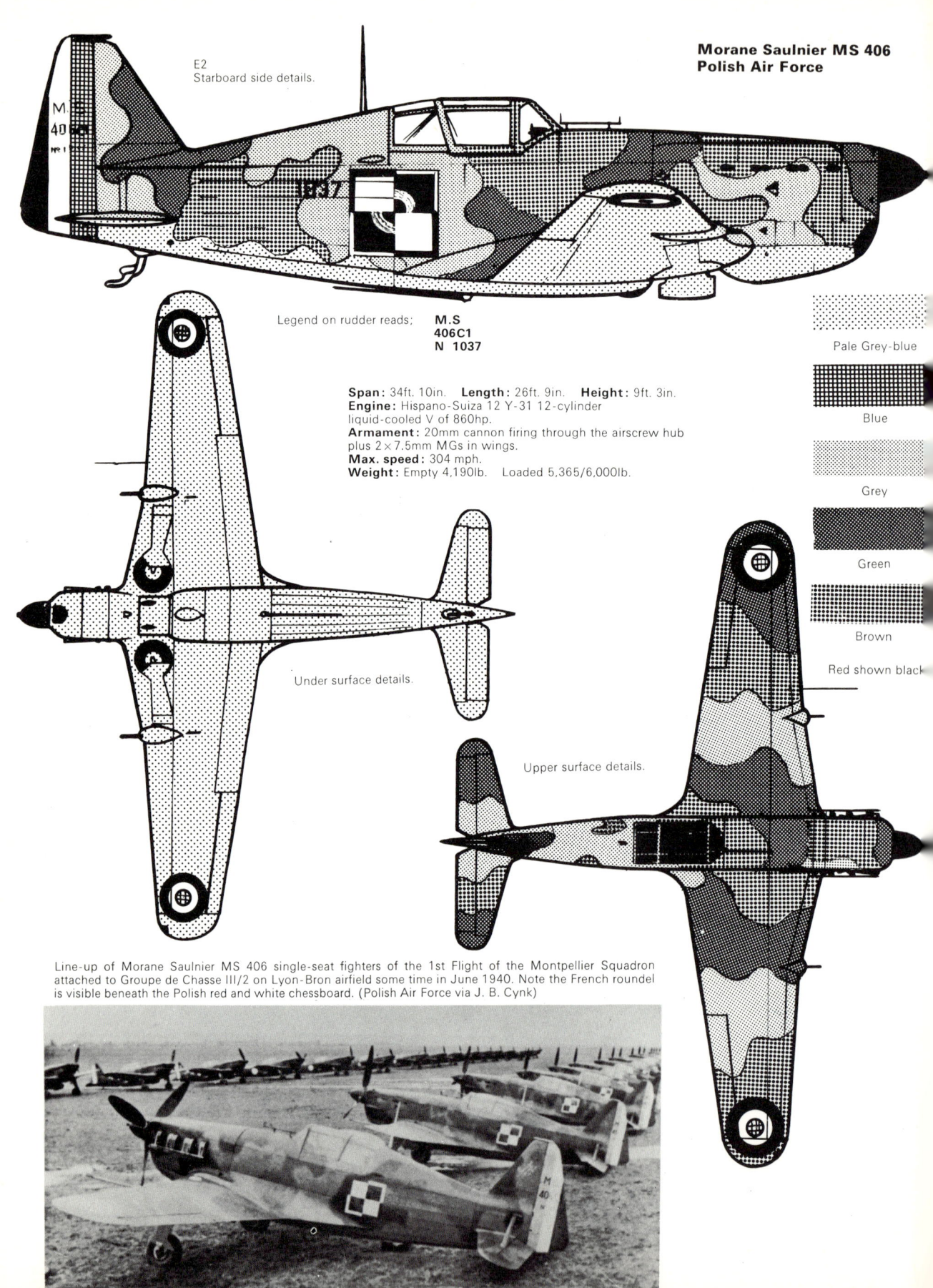

Line-up of Morane Saulnier MS 406 single-seat fighters of the 1st Flight of the Montpellier Squadron attached to Groupe de Chasse III/2 on Lyon-Bron airfield some time in June 1940. Note the French roundel is visible beneath the Polish red and white chessboard. (Polish Air Force via J. B. Cynk)

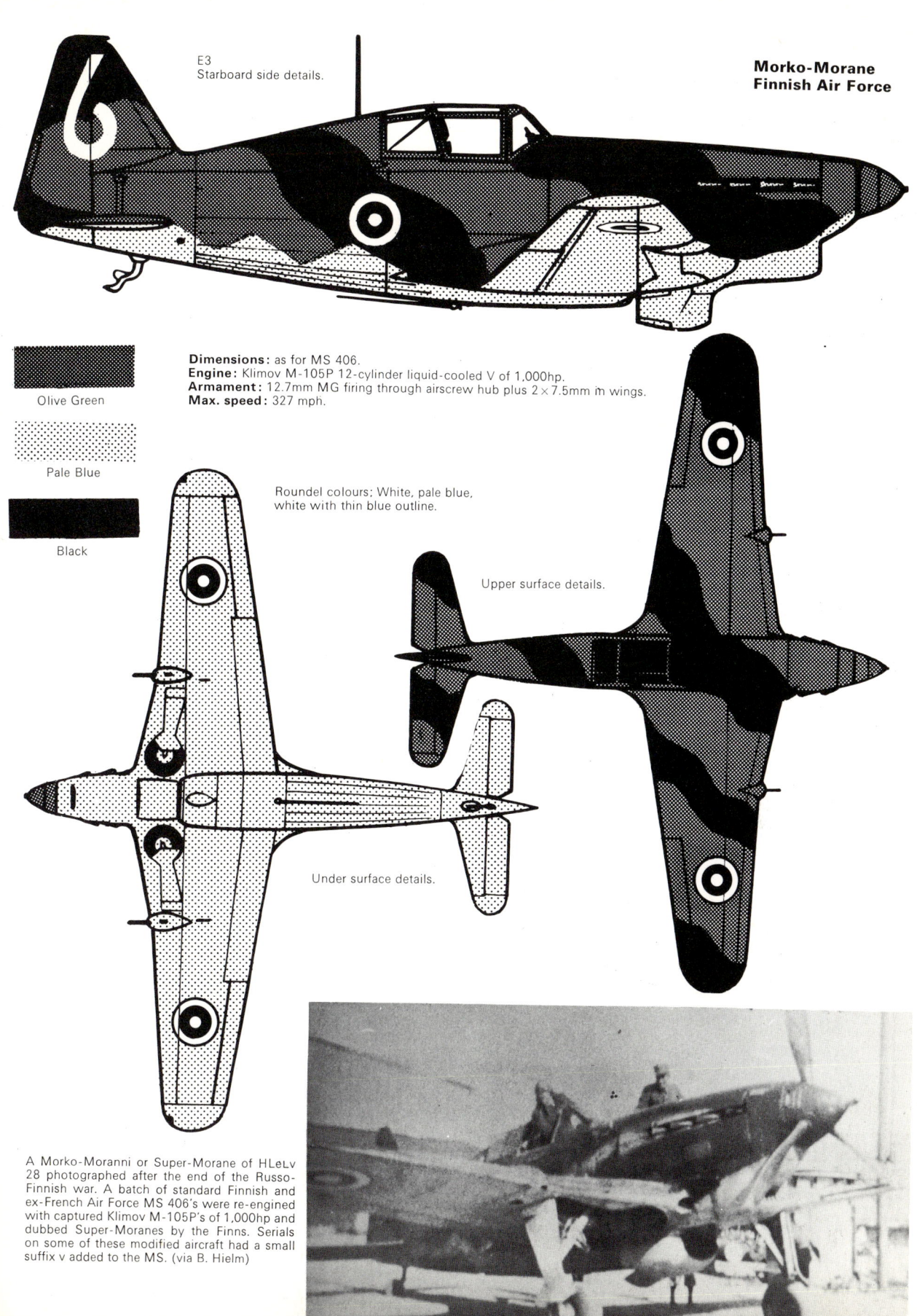

E3
Starboard side details.

**Morko-Morane
Finnish Air Force**

Olive Green

Pale Blue

Black

**Dimensions:** as for MS 406.
**Engine:** Klimov M-105P 12-cylinder liquid-cooled V of 1,000hp.
**Armament:** 12.7mm MG firing through airscrew hub plus $2 \times 7.5$mm in wings.
**Max. speed:** 327 mph.

Roundel colours: White, pale blue, white with thin blue outline.

Upper surface details.

Under surface details.

A Morko-Moranni or Super-Morane of HLeLv 28 photographed after the end of the Russo-Finnish war. A batch of standard Finnish and ex-French Air Force MS 406's were re-engined with captured Klimov M-105P's of 1,000hp and dubbed Super-Moranes by the Finns. Serials on some of these modified aircraft had a small suffix v added to the MS. (via B. Hielm)

# Mitsubishi A5M1a
# Japanese Naval Air Service

FC3
Starboard side details.

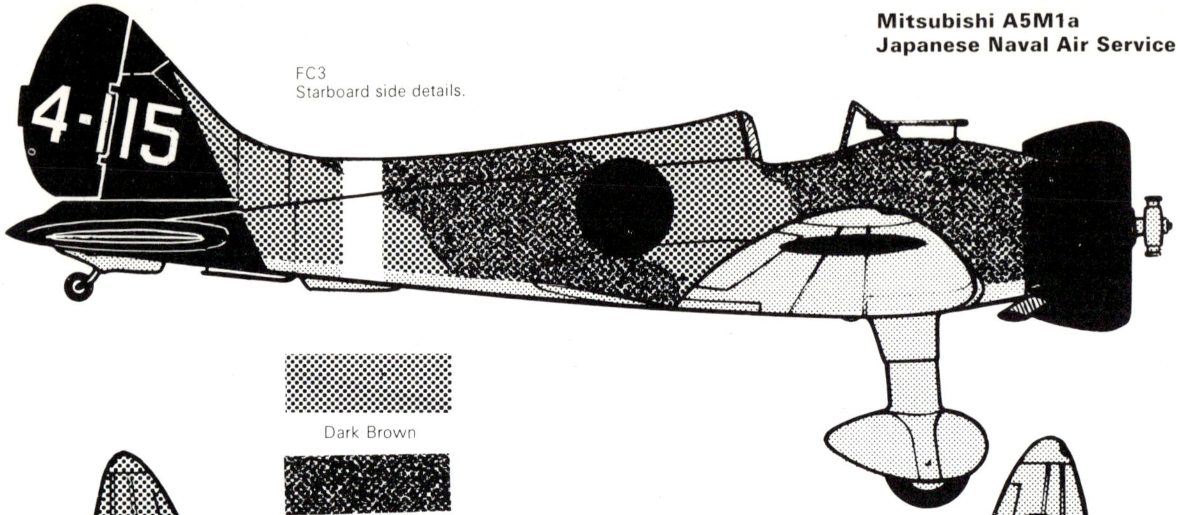

Dark Brown

Dark Green

Natural Metal

**Dimensions:** as for A5M2a.

Under surface details. Red tail unit and Hinomaru shown black. Black cowl.

Upper surface details.

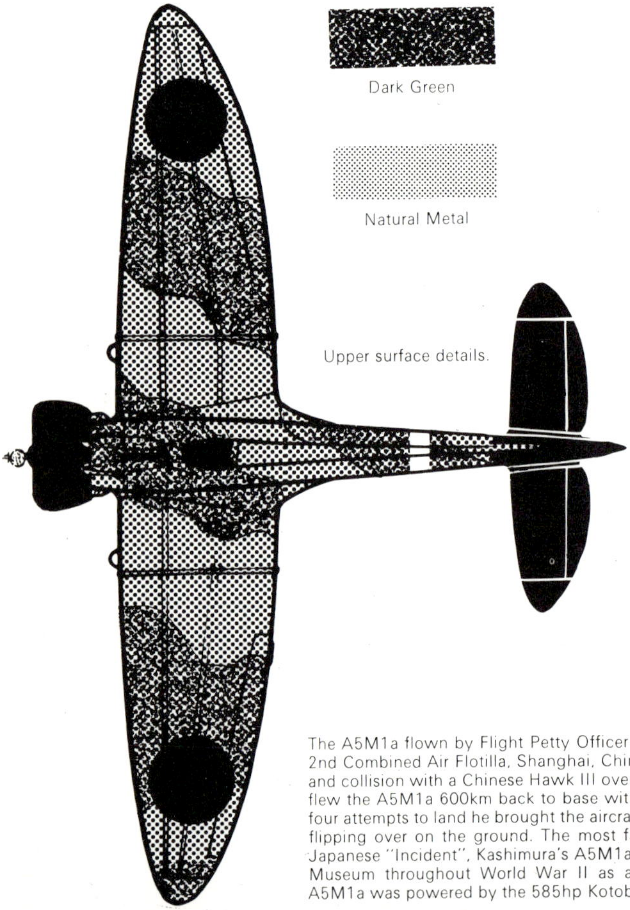

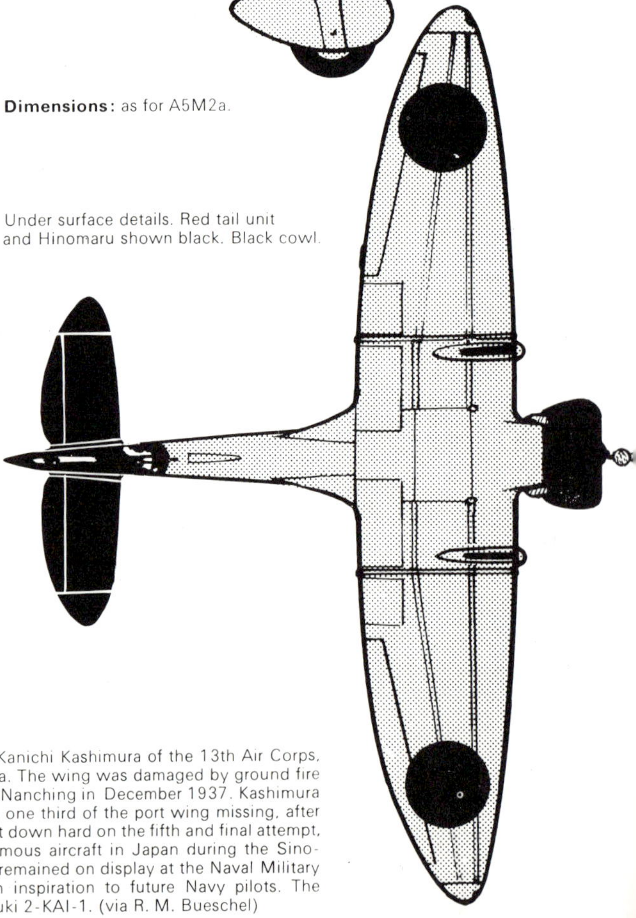

The A5M1a flown by Flight Petty Officer Kanichi Kashimura of the 13th Air Corps, 2nd Combined Air Flotilla, Shanghai, China. The wing was damaged by ground fire and collision with a Chinese Hawk III over Nanching in December 1937. Kashimura flew the A5M1a 600km back to base with one third of the port wing missing, after four attempts to land he brought the aircraft down hard on the fifth and final attempt, flipping over on the ground. The most famous aircraft in Japan during the Sino-Japanese "Incident", Kashimura's A5M1a remained on display at the Naval Military Museum throughout World War II as an inspiration to future Navy pilots. The A5M1a was powered by the 585hp Kotobuki 2-KAI-1. (via R. M. Bueschel)

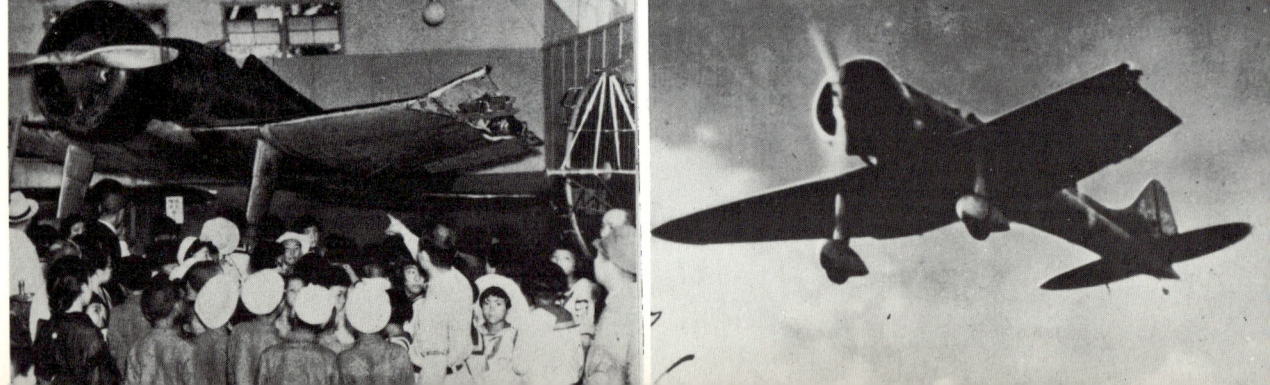

# Mitsubishi A5M2a, Type 96, Model 21
## Japanese Naval Air Service

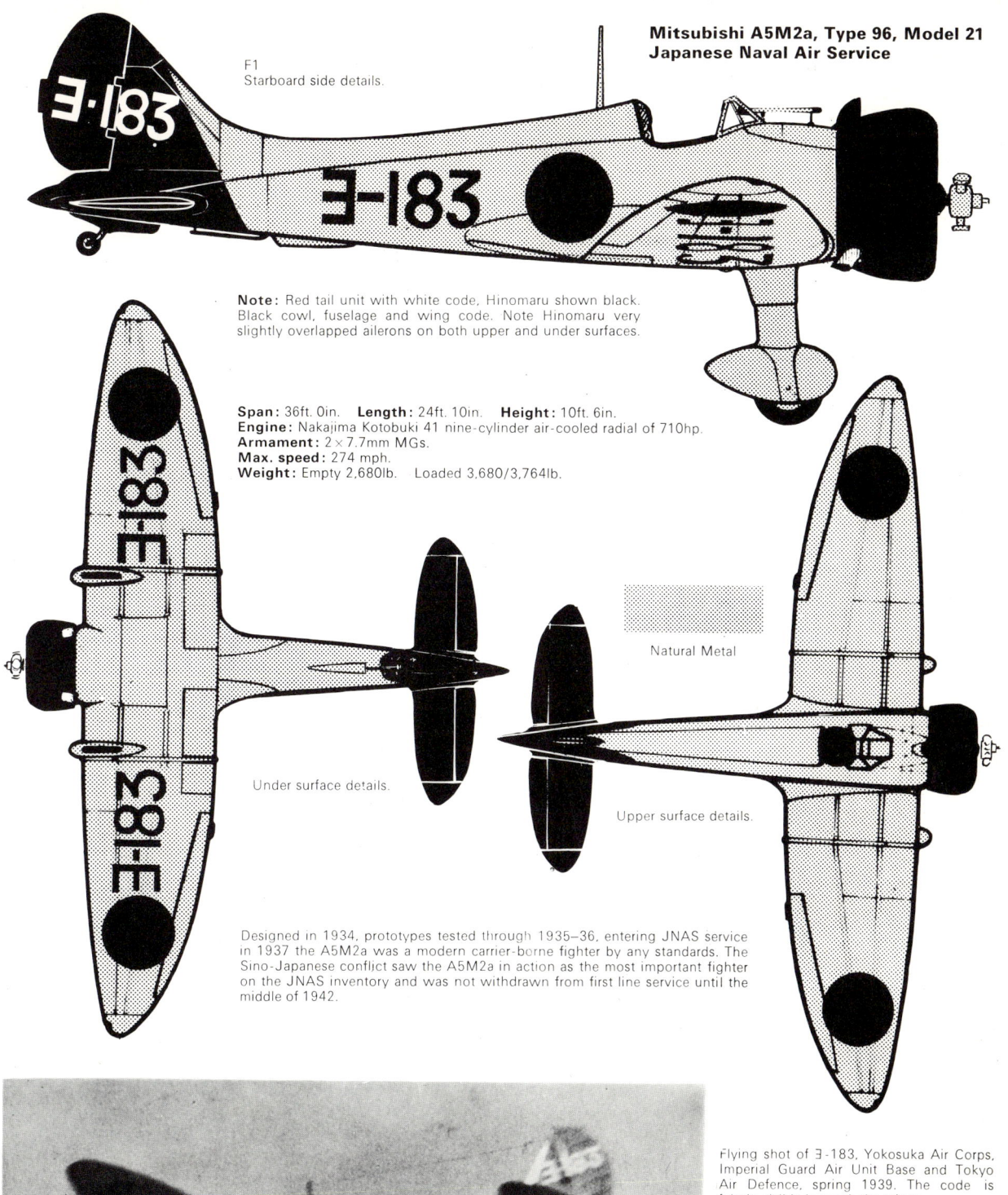

F1 Starboard side details.

**Note:** Red tail unit with white code, Hinomaru shown black. Black cowl, fuselage and wing code. Note Hinomaru very slightly overlapped ailerons on both upper and under surfaces.

**Span:** 36ft. 0in.  **Length:** 24ft. 10in.  **Height:** 10ft. 6in.
**Engine:** Nakajima Kotobuki 41 nine-cylinder air-cooled radial of 710hp.
**Armament:** 2 × 7.7mm MGs.
**Max. speed:** 274 mph.
**Weight:** Empty 2,680lb.  Loaded 3,680/3,764lb.

Natural Metal

Under surface details.

Upper surface details.

Designed in 1934, prototypes tested through 1935–36, entering JNAS service in 1937 the A5M2a was a modern carrier-borne fighter by any standards. The Sino-Japanese conflict saw the A5M2a in action as the most important fighter on the JNAS inventory and was not withdrawn from first line service until the middle of 1942.

Flying shot of ヨ-183, Yokosuka Air Corps, Imperial Guard Air Unit Base and Tokyo Air Defence, spring 1939. The code is faintly visible beneath the wings.

(via R. M. Bueschel)

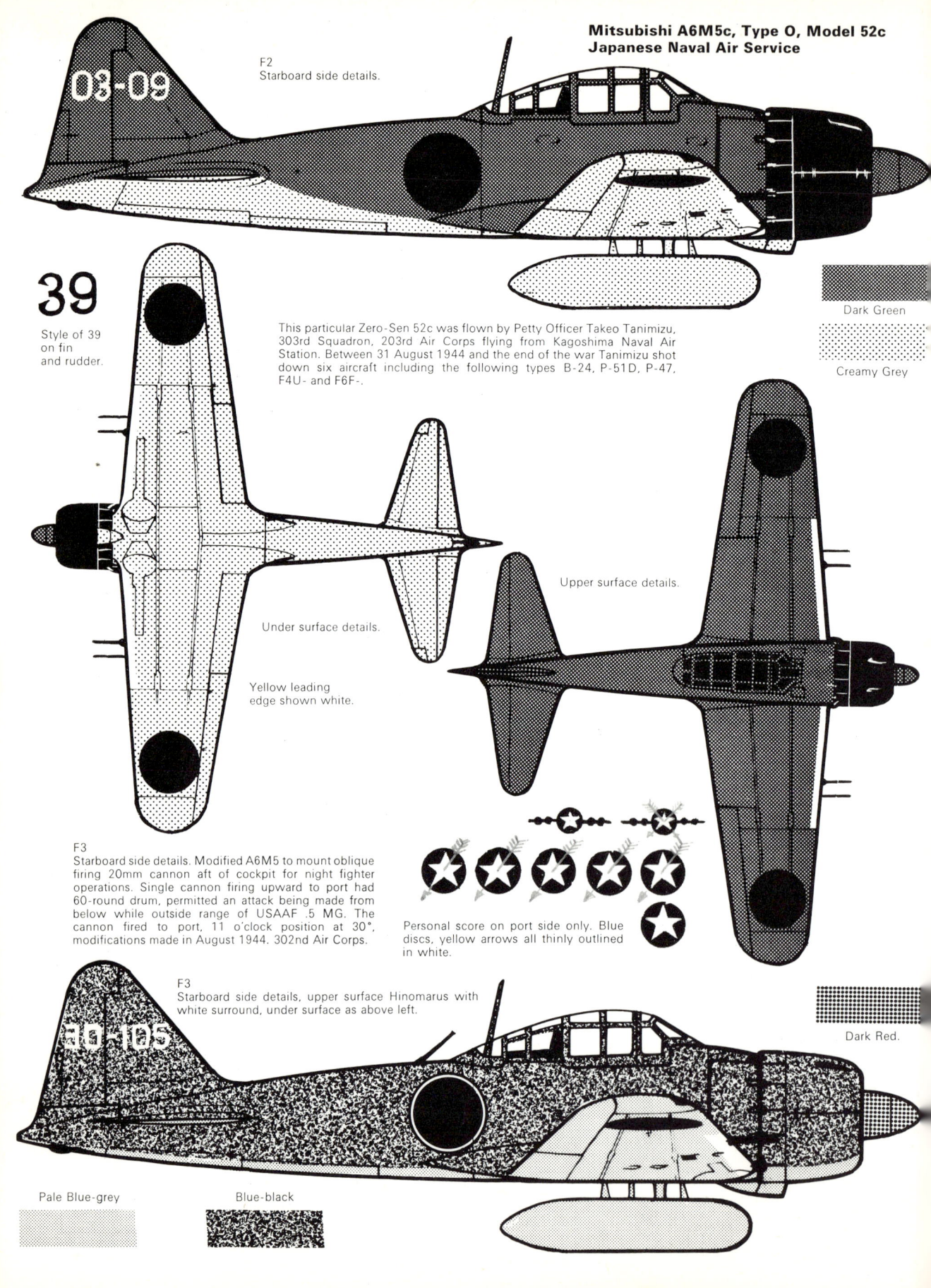

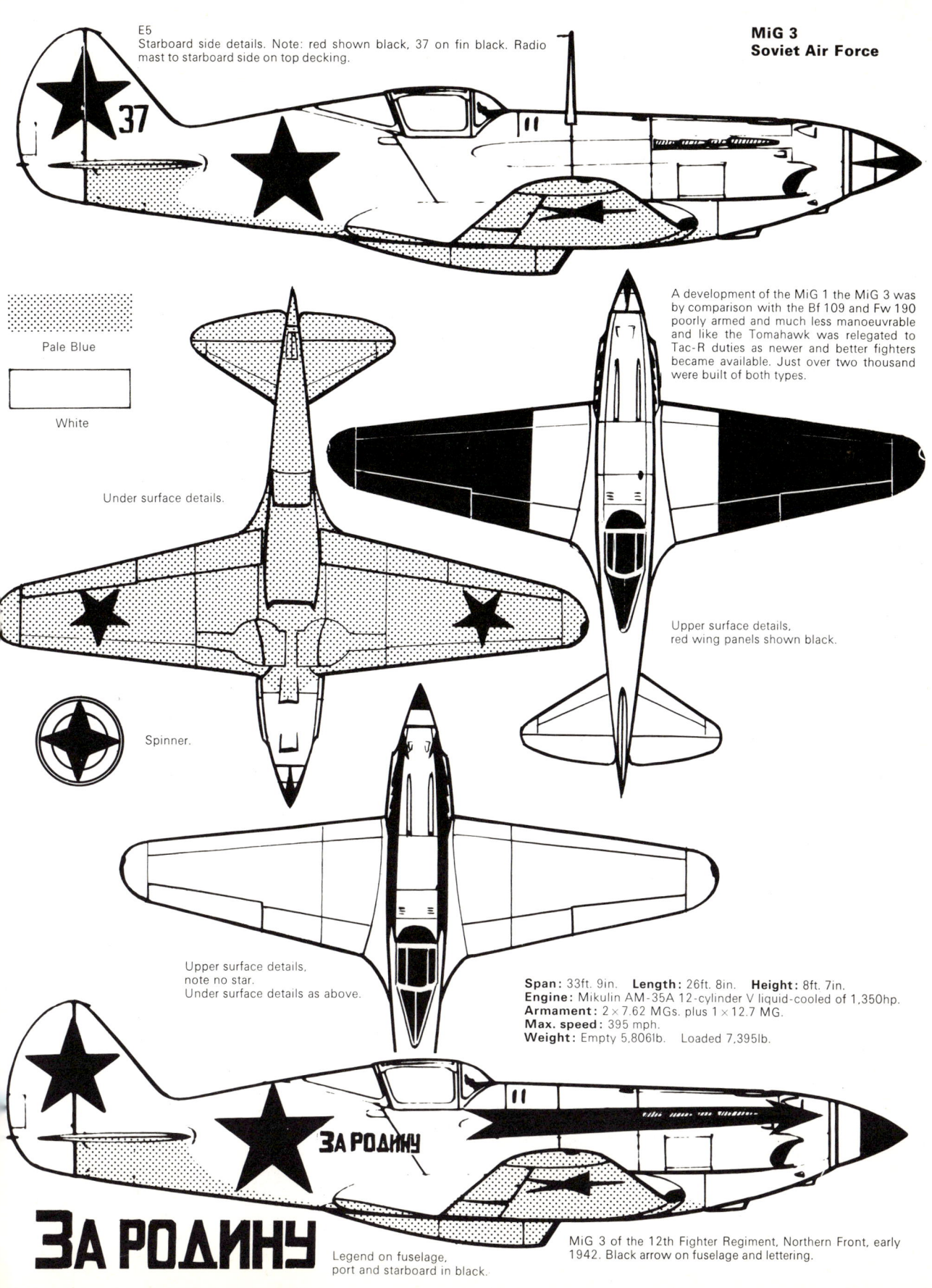

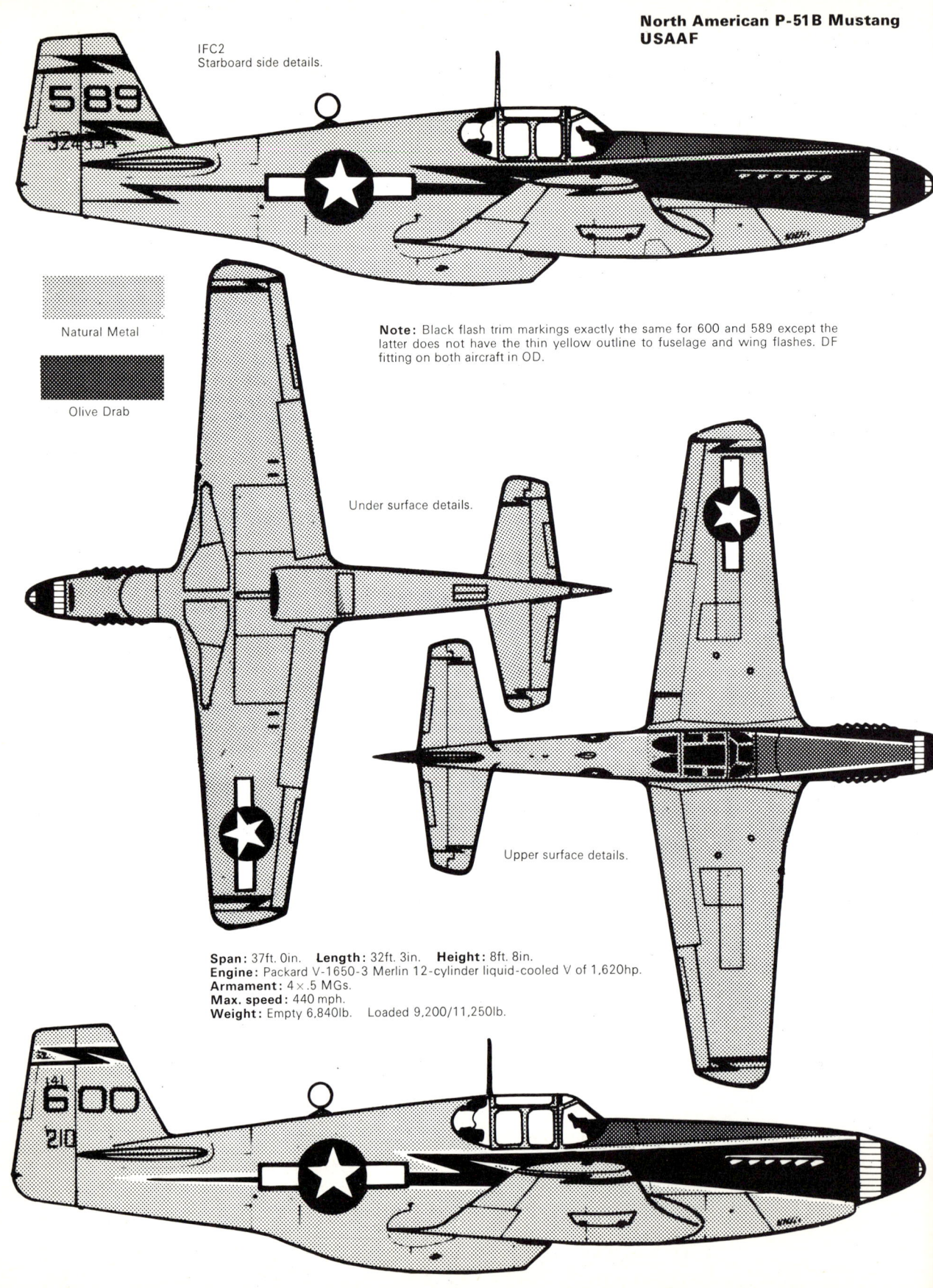

P-51B's of the 118th Tactical Reconnaissance Squadron, 14th Air Force, USAAF on Kweilin airfield, China during the last few days of the American occupation of this field before it was evacuated in the face of advancing Japanese armies. Middle photo shows 600 taking off, probably for the last time with airfield buildings burning against the rugged mountain backdrop of this field. Lower photo shows 589, note two Jap. flags under cockpit, pilots name unknown. (Photos Jack Canary via R. M. Bueschel)

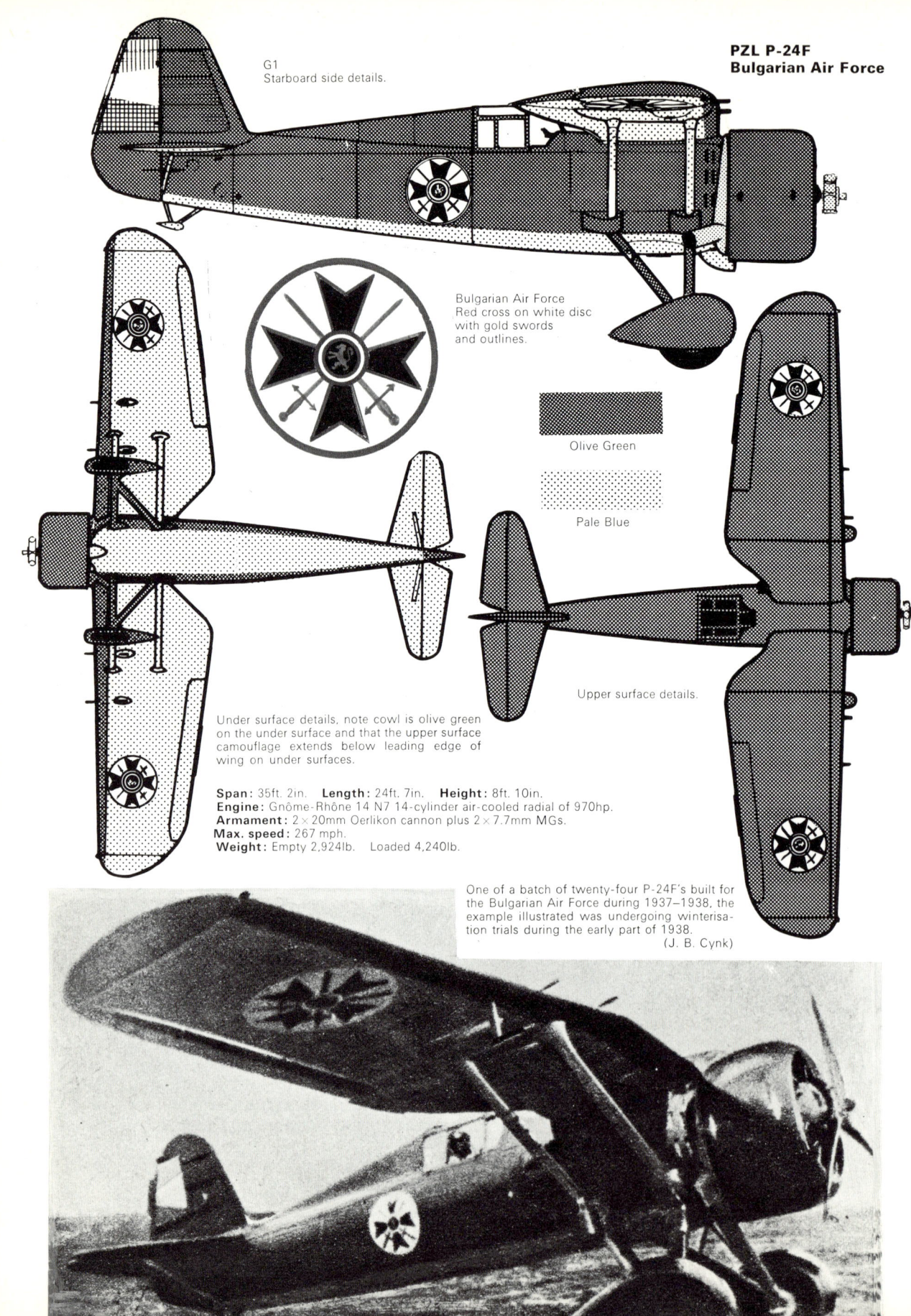

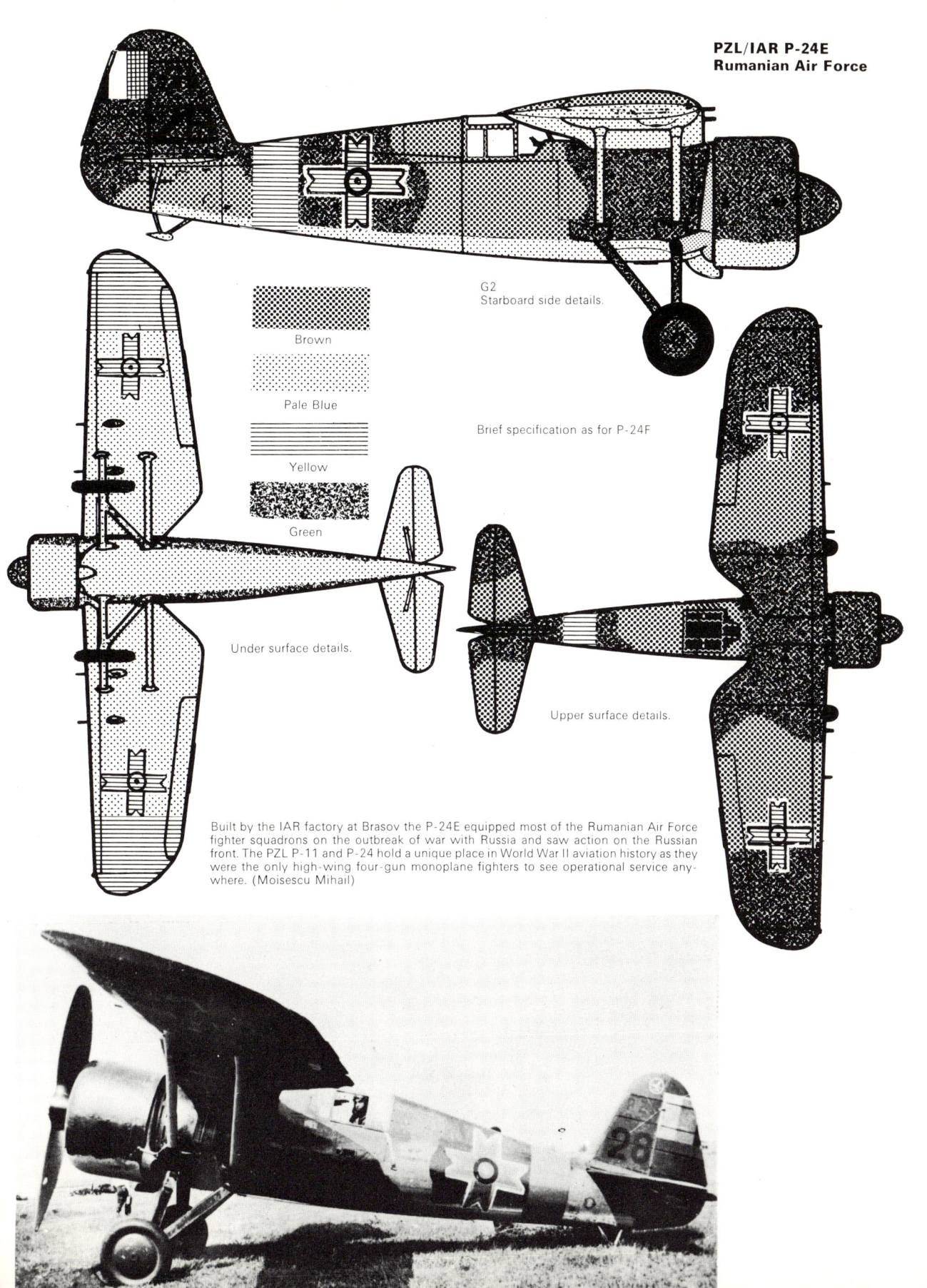

**PZL/IAR P-24E Rumanian Air Force**

G2 Starboard side details.

Brown
Pale Blue
Yellow
Green

Brief specification as for P-24F

Under surface details.

Upper surface details.

Built by the IAR factory at Brasov the P-24E equipped most of the Rumanian Air Force fighter squadrons on the outbreak of war with Russia and saw action on the Russian front. The PZL P-11 and P-24 hold a unique place in World War II aviation history as they were the only high-wing four-gun monoplane fighters to see operational service anywhere. (Moisescu Mihail)

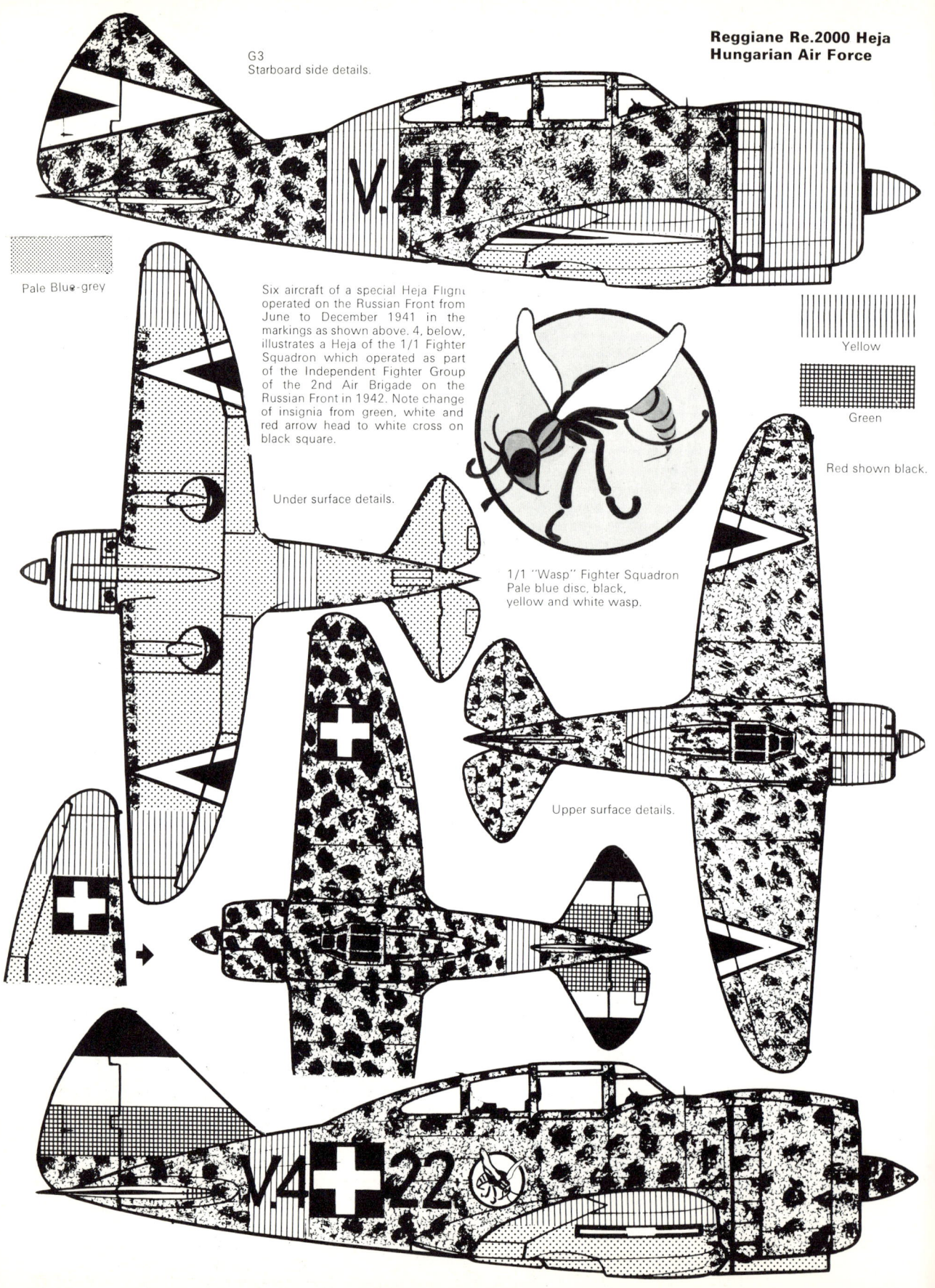

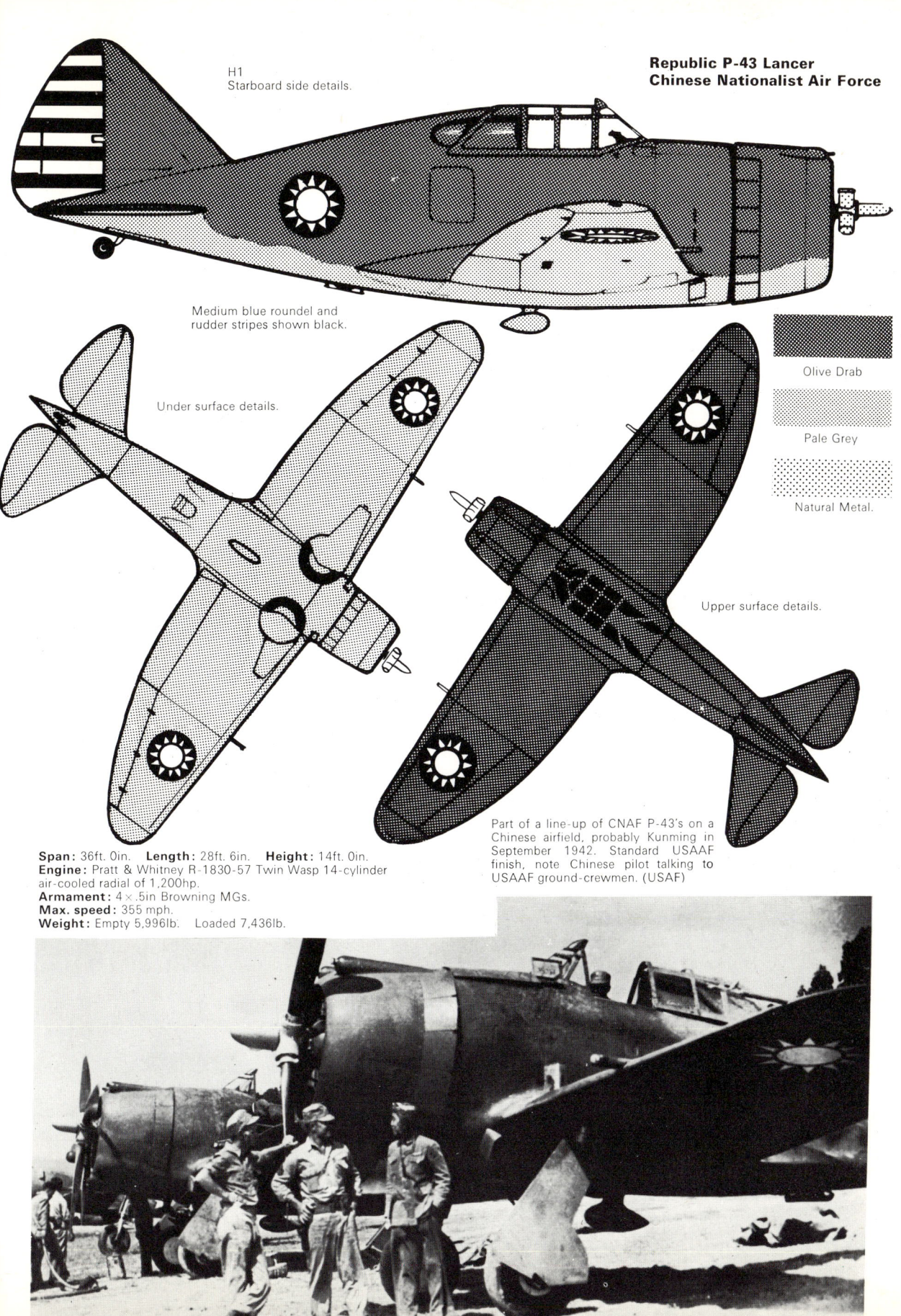

# Republic P-43 Lancer
## Chinese Nationalist Air Force

H1 Starboard side details.

Medium blue roundel and rudder stripes shown black.

Under surface details.

Olive Drab

Pale Grey

Natural Metal.

Upper surface details.

Part of a line-up of CNAF P-43's on a Chinese airfield, probably Kunming in September 1942. Standard USAAF finish, note Chinese pilot talking to USAAF ground-crewmen. (USAF)

**Span:** 36ft. 0in. **Length:** 28ft. 6in. **Height:** 14ft. 0in.
**Engine:** Pratt & Whitney R-1830-57 Twin Wasp 14-cylinder air-cooled radial of 1,200hp.
**Armament:** 4 × .5in Browning MGs.
**Max. speed:** 355 mph.
**Weight:** Empty 5,996lb. Loaded 7,436lb.

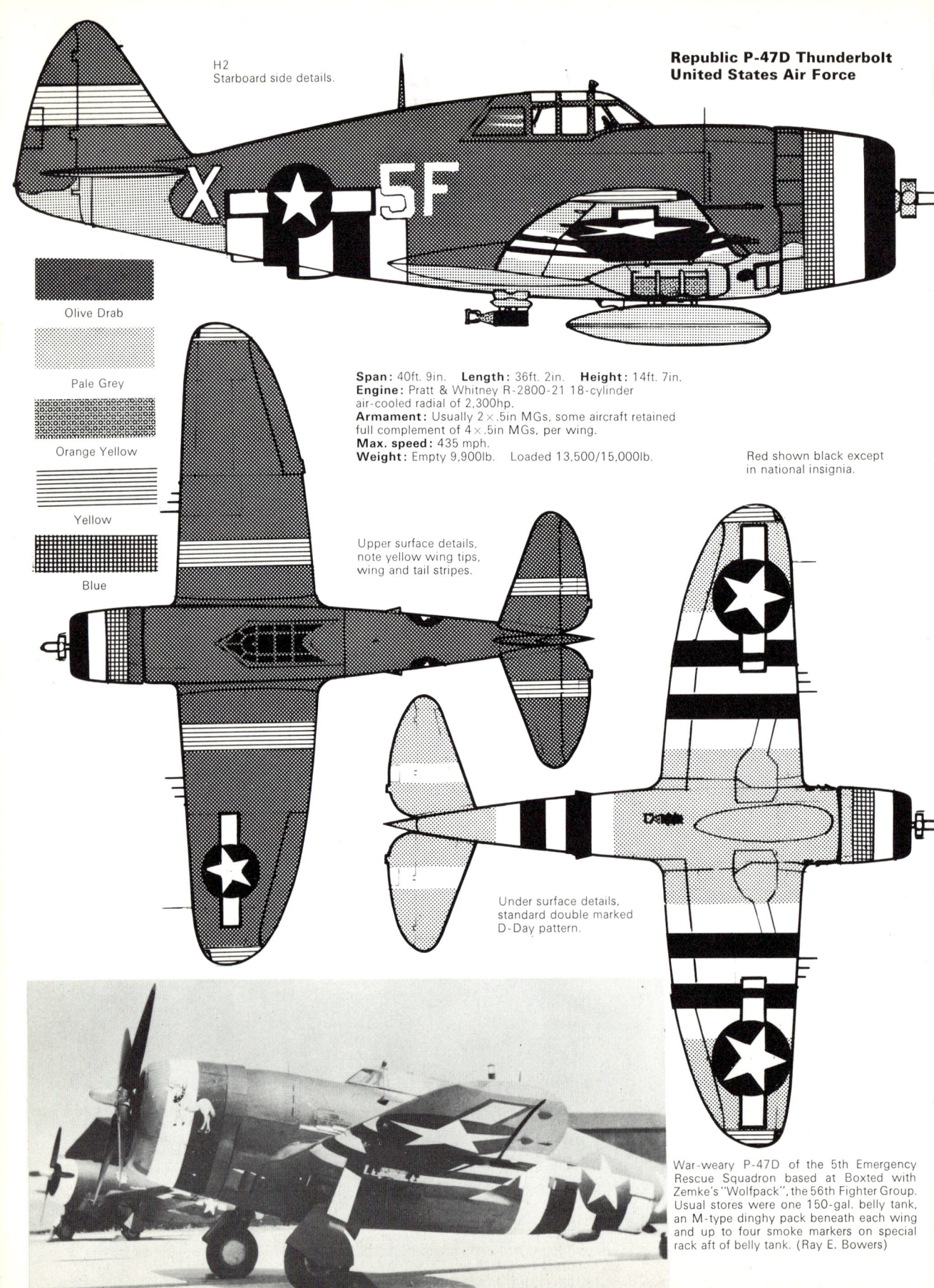

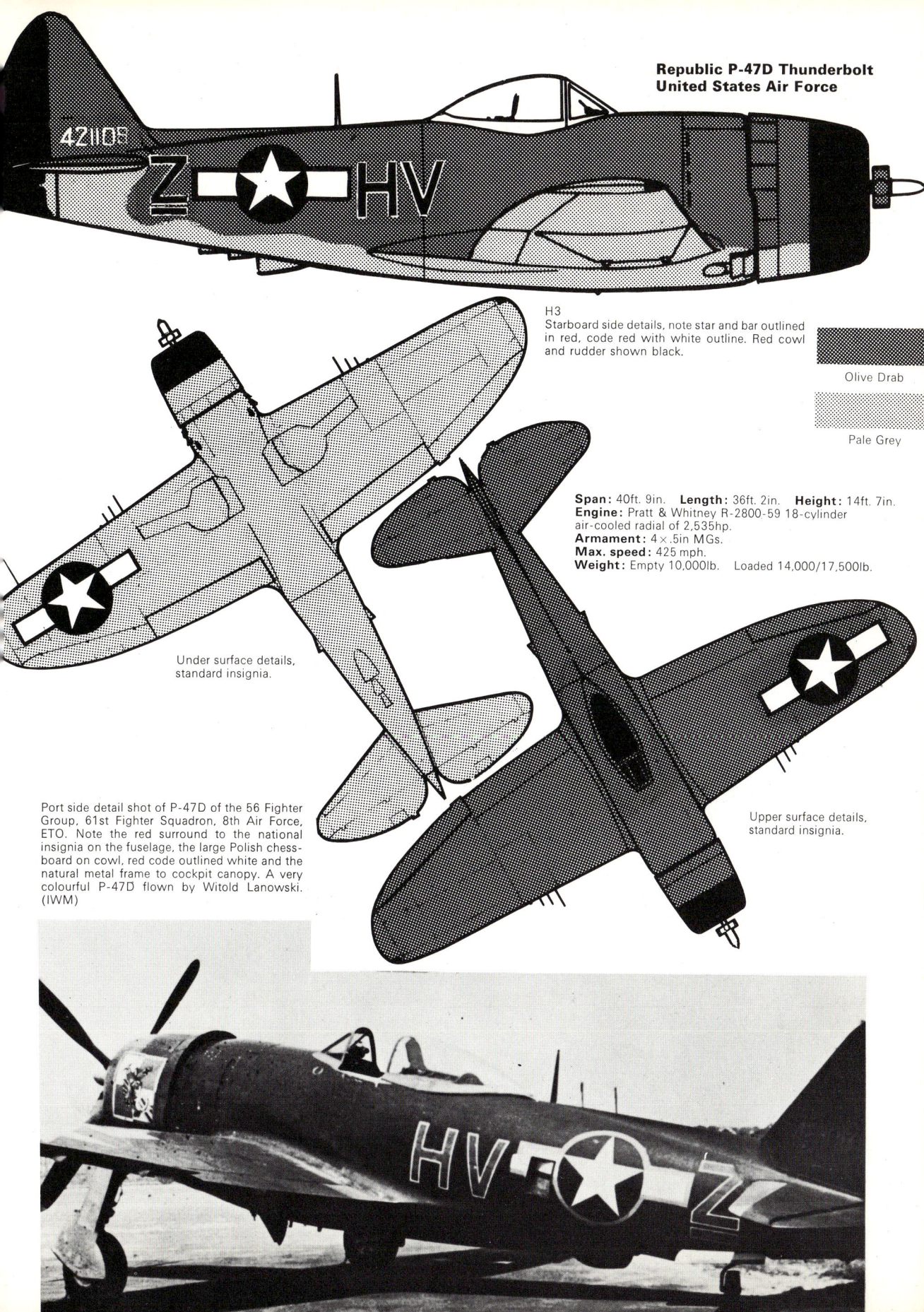

**Republic P-47D Thunderbolt**
**United States Air Force**

H3
Starboard side details, note star and bar outlined in red, code red with white outline. Red cowl and rudder shown black.

Olive Drab

Pale Grey

**Span:** 40ft. 9in. **Length:** 36ft. 2in. **Height:** 14ft. 7in.
**Engine:** Pratt & Whitney R-2800-59 18-cylinder air-cooled radial of 2,535hp.
**Armament:** 4 × .5in MGs.
**Max. speed:** 425 mph.
**Weight:** Empty 10,000lb. Loaded 14,000/17,500lb.

Under surface details, standard insignia.

Upper surface details, standard insignia.

Port side detail shot of P-47D of the 56 Fighter Group, 61st Fighter Squadron, 8th Air Force, ETO. Note the red surround to the national insignia on the fuselage, the large Polish chessboard on cowl, red code outlined white and the natural metal frame to cockpit canopy. A very colourful P-47D flown by Witold Lanowski. (IWM)

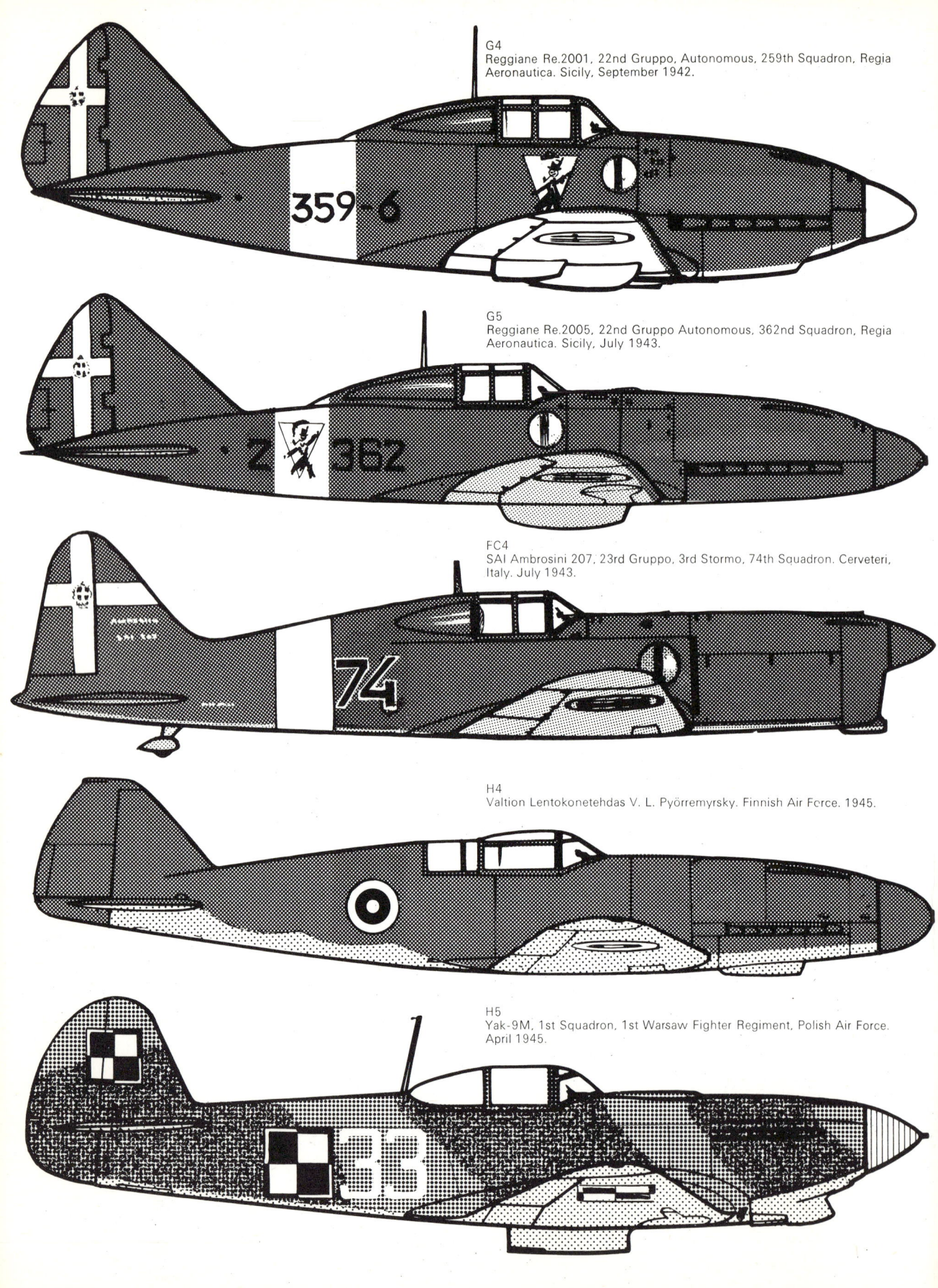

G4
Reggiane Re.2001, 22nd Gruppo, Autonomous, 259th Squadron, Regia Aeronautica. Sicily, September 1942.

G5
Reggiane Re.2005, 22nd Gruppo Autonomous, 362nd Squadron, Regia Aeronautica. Sicily, July 1943.

FC4
SAI Ambrosini 207, 23rd Gruppo, 3rd Stormo, 74th Squadron. Cerveteri, Italy. July 1943.

H4
Valtion Lentokonetehdas V. L. Pyörremyrsky. Finnish Air Force. 1945.

H5
Yak-9M, 1st Squadron, 1st Warsaw Fighter Regiment, Polish Air Force. April 1945.